The Descendants of John Meridy Turner (1747–1815) of Fauquier County, Virginia

Gwen Boyer Bjorkman

HERITAGE BOOKS
2014

HERITAGE BOOKS
AN IMPRINT OF HERITAGE BOOKS, INC.

Books, CDs, and more—Worldwide

For our listing of thousands of titles see our website
at
www.HeritageBooks.com

Published 2014 by
HERITAGE BOOKS, INC.
Publishing Division
5810 Ruatan Street
Berwyn Heights, Md. 20740

Heritage Books by the author:

Pasquotank County, North Carolina Record of Deed, 1700–1751

Quaker Marriage Certificates: Concord Monthly Meeting, Delaware County, Pennsylvania, 1679–1808

Quaker Marriage Certificates: New Garden Monthly Meeting, Chester County, Pennsylvania, 1704–1799

Quaker Marriage Certificates: Pasquotank, Perquimans, Piney Woods, and Suttons Creek Monthly Meetings, North Carolina, 1677–1800

The Descendants of John Meridy Turner (1747–1815) of Fauquier County, Virginia

CD: Pasquotank County, North Carolina Record of Deeds, 1700–1751

CD: Quaker Marriage Certificates

International Standard Book Numbers
Paperbound: 978-0-7884-0145-9
Clothbound: 978-0-7884-6067-8

This Book is Dedicated

to the Descendants of

CHARLES DANIEL TURNER

Mary Turner Evans and Harriet Turner Beeman

Two of the Daughters of Charles Daniel Turner

CONTENTS

MAPS and TABLES

PREFACE

Since the name TURNER is so common and can be found everywhere in Great Britain and even on the continent of Europe, there is no common progenitor for all the families of this surname. It is classified as a "trade" name, similar to Smith, Wright, Carpenter, Thatcher and Cooper. Originally a "turner" was one who worked with a lathe.

There were therefore many unrelated TURNER families in the early American Colonies. This book is limited to the descendants of John Meridy TURNER, son of William TURNER. The earliest TURNER families in Fauquier County, Virginia were William, Edward and James TURNER with their Leases for Three Lives in 1746. William TURNER'S lease was for the term of his life and the lives of his two sons, John Meridy and William. The lease was to last as long as one of the three was still living.

We have not been able to trace the other son, William TURNER. However, there was a William TURNER living in Culpeper County who died in the Revolutionary War and left a small family.[1]

The families of Edward and James TURNER, who also had Leases for Three Lives in 1746, are not yet proven. Edward TURNER, who died about 1805 in Fauquier County and left a large family is being researched.[2] He may be the son of Edward named in his lease. James TURNER, who married Kerenhappuck NORMAN about 1733, may be the elder James TURNER of the Lease for Three Lives. This James TURNER is found in Spotsylvania and Culpeper Counties. His family left the area for Halifax County, Virginia, between 1750 and 1760.[3]

There were at least three other unrelated TURNER families in Fauquier County during the same time period that our John Meridy TURNER was living there.

First, there was the family of Col. Thomas TURNER of King George County who left property in Fauquier County to his grandsons, Major Thomas TURNER and Turner DIXON in 1758.[4]

Second, Fielding TURNER of Fairfax County had a son Pierce TURNER who died in Culpeper County in 1803 and had a son John

TURNER who married Frankey JONES in 1798 in Fauquier County.[5]

Third, there were two grandsons of Edward TURNER of St. Mary's County, Maryland, Hezekiah and Zephaniah TURNER, who lived in Fauquier and Culpeper Counties after about 1767.[6]

Also, there was an Edward TURNER who died in 1719 in Talbot County, Maryland who was married to Sarah MEREDITH, daughter of John MEREDITH. They had sons named William and Edward who apparently remained in Maryland.[7] The coincidence of the name John MEREDITH with our John Meridy TURNER, son of William TURNER has been a topic of research.

Research on the TURNER family has extended over the last 28 years and it is now time to get something about this family written down for future generations to work on. It has always been regretted that we cannot prove the immigrant ancestor on this line.

My thanks are extended to Dave MARTIN who has been the source of much of this research over the years. His publishing of the *Martin Family History* for their family reunion in 1982 has been the basis for this work. Thanks are also due to Emalie Fletcher EWING who wrote *My Turner Family* in 1969 and shared a copy with me. Her research in the Missouri records was so helpful.

The genealogical section of the book is presented in the Modified Register format. Each generation can be traced by the number assigned. Only TURNERS and TURNER daughters are traced in the next generation and indicated by a "+". The father's name and number is given in parentheses after each numbered name in order to trace back to the previous generation. Geographic locations are given as town, county, state. If there are only two locations, it is the county and state. In the End Notes for each chapter, U. S. Census references are not usually given. Where a film number is given, it is from the Family History Library in Salt Lake City, Utah, unless otherwise noted.

I hope you will all enjoy this story of our family.

Gwen Boyer Bjorkman
Bellevue, Washington
February, 1994

NOTES: PREFACE

1 "British Mercantile Claims 1775-1803," *The Virginia Genealogist* (1984) 28:114.

2 Correspondence with Jean Smidt, 7725 Warwick Ave, Darien, IL 60561 (1993); Paul T. Davis, III, 460 E. Ventris Lane, Maitland, FL 32751 (1971).

3 David W. Martin, *Martin Family History* (Boyds, MD, 1982, 1993), pp. 1-2; John Motley Morehead III, *The Morehead Family of North Carolina and Virginia* (New York, 1921), pp. 37-43, 108-110.

4 "The Turner Family of King George County," *Virginia Magazine of History and Biography* (Oct 1912, Jan-Oct 1913) 20:438-440, 21:106-109, 211; John K. Gott & T. Triplett Russell, *The Dixon Valley, Its First 250 Years* (Bowie, MD: Heritage Books, 1991); Film #92440 Item #5, TURNER FAMILY.

5 Shirley J. Turner, "Ancestors and Descendants of Fielding Turner: England, Ireland, Virginia, North Carolina and Missouri," (Tucson, AZ, 1983) [Paper submitted to the Family History Writing Contest of the National Genealogical Society in 1983]; Film #92440 Item #5, TURNER FAMILY.

6 Willetta Baylis Blum and William Blum, Sr., *The Baylis Family of Virginia* (Washington, D.C., 1958), pp. 421-431.

7 Henry Chandlee Forman, *The Turner Family of Hebron and Betterton, Maryland* (Baltimore, MD: Waverly Press, 1933).

THE DESCENDANTS OF JOHN MERIDY TURNER (1747-1815) OF FAUQUIER COUNTY, VIRGINIA

CHAPTER I

THE FIRST GENERATION

John Meridy TURNER was a Virginian. His family had probably been in Virginia for at least four generations, but left few records. It seems impossible now to prove who was our immigrant ancestor. The people of Fauquier County shared a common English background. They had come mainly from the lower tidewater counties of the Northern Neck of Virginia. Land, by far, was the prime motive prompting immigration to Virginia, yet few owned land.

> "Fauquier was an area of many leases of land due to much of it being owned by a few individuals in a proprietorship or a large grant, which they divided and leased in small parcels to others. This caused a restlessness among the settlers, so many moved on elsewhere when they were unable to buy the land that they farmed. They went over into the Shenandoah Valley, out to Ohio and down into the Carolinas."[1]

The territory lying between the Potomac and Rappahannock Rivers is historically known as the Northern Neck. Consisting of 5,282,000 acres, the Northern Neck land was granted in 1649 to seven supporters of Charles II, the exiled son of the executed Charles I. By 1681 Lord Thomas CULPEPER, son of one of the original patentees, purchased the rights of the other patentees and became the sole proprietor of the Northern Neck. On his death, the land passed to his daughter, then to her son, Lord Thomas FAIRFAX. It became known as the Fairfax grant. This was the largest estate ever owned by an individual in this country. Starting in 1690, grants were issued by agents of the Proprietary and the records were maintained separately from the grants in the rest of the Colony.[2]

Northumberland County was formed about 1645 from the Chickacoan District, the region between the Potomac and Rappahannock Rivers set aside as an Indian reserve. Many of the early settlers were from Maryland. Northumberland reached its present size in 1653, after the creation of Westmoreland County.[3] The most likely candidate for our immigrant ancestor seems to be a John TURNER of Northumberland County who had a son John TURNER born 2 December 1671 and baptized at St. Stephens

Parish. There was also an Edward TURNER, son to Jo'n, baptized 14 May 1693, at St. Stephens Parish, Northumberland County.[4]

In this same parish register were people with the name spelled MERIDEY, MERRYDAY, MEREDY or MEREDITH. As early as 1656 there was a marriage record for a John MERRYDAY and Mrs. Ann NASH, alias MALLETT.[5] In this paper we have used the variant spellings: John <u>Meridy</u> TURNER(1), Daniel <u>Meridy</u> TURNER(4), and John <u>Meredith</u> TURNER(7), because records were found with these spellings. It appears to be all variations of the same name.

The first TURNER record found in Westmoreland County was in 1694 when Edward TURNER was a plaintiff against Wm. STRATFIELD. The case was dismissed 30 August 1694.[6] In the Westmoreland County Deeds, "Edward TURNER gives for his mark of cattle and hoggs a crop, a slit and an underkeele on each ear. 28 Nov. 1707."[7]

In the Westmoreland County Wills there was a will for Sarah PALMER, dated 2 March 1717 and proved 25 June 1718. She named a daughter Sarah, wife of Edward TURNER and granddaughters, Sarah and Jane TURNER.[8]

One or more of the above records for Edward TURNER may be the same man as the Edward TURNER of St. Stephens Parish who wrote his will on 22 February 1737/8, proved 10 April 1738, in Northumberland County. His wife was "to have and keep all her goods and chattles that she had when I married her." The children named were:

> Sons: William TURNER and Edward TURNER to have all my tract of land in Westmoreland County, to be equally divided between them.
>
> Daughter: Mary TURNER to have household items.

The rest of the estate was to be divided between his five children: William, Edwin, Mary, John and Elizabeth TURNER.

"Sons William, Edwin, and daughter Mary TURNER to live on the plantation above mentioned, and also my son John and daughter Elizabeth if they think fit. They shall not have the liberty to make any bargains or to sell or buy anything without advice and consent of their Uncle William GARNER, and I appoint my friend William GARNER executor." The witnesses were John TURNER and Rebecca GARNER.[9]

It appears that the name of Edward was written in error as "Edwin" in the will. Oftentimes there were errors by the copyist who recorded the will. But our interest now turns to the son William TURNER named in the will. The uncle William GARNER would seem to be the same person who died in 1751 in Northumberland and his estate was appraised by John WEST, Pemberton CLAUGHTON and John TURNER. This may then be the same John TURNER who witnessed the will of Edward TURNER in 1738.[10]

John GARNER, founder of this GARNER family, came to Northumberland County in 1650 at the age of 17. The uncle William GARNER of the will was the grandson of John GARNER. Joseph GARNER, brother of the above William GARNER, on 11 July 1737 transferred to Edward TURNER 150 acres lying in the Forrest of Yeocomoco and Mochotick, Cople Parish, Westmoreland County, "within the bounds of a Proprietor's Deed for 390 acres, dated 10th January 1709, granted John GARNER late of the afsd. county deceased, father of Joseph and Bequeathed Joseph by will of 3 February 1712."[11] This may be the same land that Edward TURNER then willed to his sons William and Edward in February of 1737/8.

Another son of the founder, Henry GARNER, had a will written in Westmoreland County in 1744 and proved in 1745 that was witnessed by William TURNER and Peter RUST.[12] The name of Edward TURNER and Peter RUST were found on a Rent Roll for Westmoreland County for Cople Parish for the Year 1740.[13] A List of Voters in the 1741 Burgess Election from Westmoreland County included William TURNER and Peter RUST. The law enacted in 1736 provided that any man in order to vote must own at least 100 acres of land, if no settlement was made on it, and at least 25 acres if settled with a house and plantation.[14]

King George County was formed in 1721 from Richmond County. Part of King George went toward the creation of Prince William County in 1731. Many of the early records of King George County are missing. This is the connection for our TURNER family that cannot be proven. To summarize, we have the William TURNER who inherited the land in Westmoreland County from his father, Edward TURNER, in 1738, he was a voter in 1741, and witness to a will in 1744. Then in 1745 Wm. X TURNER and John MCCORMIC were witnesses to the will of Mary GINNINGS [JENNINGS] in King George County.[15]

In 1715 Nathaniel HEDGMAN received a grant of 750 acres "on the north side of Rappahannock River about 35 miles above the falls thereof," and his sons, Peter and Nathaniel, Jr., in August, 1724, increased the family holdings to 4,800 acres by each taking grants of 2,025 acres, described as "on the north side of Rappahannock River opposite to the little ford and adjoining the land of Nathaniel dec'd." (A:61, 62) The North Fork of the Rappahannock was soon to become known by HEDGMAN'S name and the quarter established by his sons between Tin Pot Run and the river below the mouth of Great Run, survived as a landmark on many maps.[16]

Most of these grants were in the nature of frontier land speculations by tidewater landholders who had no intention at the time of becoming residents of the new country, nor, in many cases, of establishing slave quarters. If a "quarter" was settled as a tobacco plantation, the owner erected buildings and established an overseer with slaves under him to cultivate the land.[17]

In 1747 there was recorded in Prince William County three leases for three lives (each for 200 acres) from Peter HEDGMAN. The first lease dated February 1745 was for the lives of Edward TURNER and his sons James TURNER and Edward TURNER. The second lease dated 26 May 1746 was for the lives of William TURNER and his sons William TURNER and <u>John Meridy</u> TURNER. The third lease dated February 1745 was for the lives of James TURNER his son James TURNER and his daughter Mary TURNER. The leases were found recorded together in the Prince William County deed book and the land of William and Edward was adjoining. James TURNER witnessed Edward's lease. Edward TURNER witnessed James' lease. William TURNER'S lease for three lives on HEDGMAN [Rappahannock] River was beginning at Edward TURNER'S corner.[18]

The town of Remington now stands on part of Edward TURNER'S lease. Today, US Route 29 going south from Warrenton to Culpeper as it bridges the Rappahannock River goes over the same land that was leased by our William TURNER.[19] This lease for three lives proves that our <u>John Meridy</u> TURNER was the son of William TURNER.

Here is a transcription of this lease recorded in Prince William County Virginia Deed Book I:70:

"**Hedgman** gent. to **Turner** Lease for Lives Sept. 25 1747 Dd **Wm. Turner**

This indenture made this xxvith day of May in the year of our Lord one thousand seven hundred and forty six Between **Peter Hedgman** of the county of Stafford gent. of the one part & **William Turner** of the county of Prince William planter of the other part Witnesseth that the said **Peter Hedgman** hath devised granted set and to farm let & by these presents doth devise act and to farm let one messuage tenement & tract of land situate lying & being in the said county of Prince William & on the north east side of Rappahannock river about two miles below the mouth of Hedgman river & bounded as follow, to wit, beginning at **Edward Turners** corner red oak on ye river side & extending with his line N 35° E 207 Po to a swamp oak being another corner tree of the said **Turners** land & also a corner tree to the land leased to **William Cagi** thence N 20° W 80 po and a half to a corner white oak sapling thence S 75° W 260 po to a corner red oak sapling about two poles from the sd river thence up it about 8 po to include a spring thence down the said river according to its several courses to the beginning containing two hundred acres more or less to the said **William Turner** his heirs & assigns for and in consideration of the rents and duties hereafter mentioned & for & during the term and space of the natural lives of him the sd **William Turner** his son **William** & his son **John Meridy** together with all houses outhouses gardens orchards woods under woods waters water courses profits commodities & appurtenances whatsoever thereunto belonging or in anywise appurtaining To have and to hold the said messuage tenement tract or parcel of land with the appurtenances to him the said **William Turner** his heirs & assigns for and during the natural lives of him the said **William** his son **William** & his son **John Meridy** or the longest liver of them Yielding & paying yearly and every year during the space and term afd unto the said **Peter Hedgman** his heirs or assigns on the 18th day of October being the feastday of St. Luke the Evangelist of the growth of the said plantation the neat sum and quantity of one thousand pounds of good merchantable Tobacco and cask and the quitrents of the said land & the said **William Turner** doth agree for himself his heirs Exrs Admrs. & assigns to plant a good sufficient orchard of apple trees within five years of the date hereof to consist of 100 at a proper & of convenient distance & to fence in & preserve the same from the hurt of creatures and as any of them destroy to plant others in their stead and only to trim and guard them & at the expiration of the aforesaid term to leave the sd orchard in good repair and the tenant with convenient houses & good sufficient fencing thereon in good order & repair & fit & convenient in every manner for another tenant to enter upon and possess the same also that no subtenant shall be taken thereon during the above mentioned term under the penalty of one thousand pounds of good merchantable tobacco & cask over and above the above described yearly rent and that the said **William** his heirs & Exrs Admrs or assigns or either of them shall not sell make over or transfer the sd tract of land to any person or persons whatsoever without the asent & approbation first obtained in writing of the said **Peter Hedgman** his heirs & assigns under the penalty of £50 sterl. & the forfeiture of this Lease & its further covenants & agreed upon by and between the said parties that the said **William Turner** his heirs and assigns shall not during the said term do make commit or cause to be done made or remitted any manner of waste or in and upon the said demised premises or any part thereof during the said term except what is used for building fencing & other edifices belonging to the said plantation or tenement & for necessary firewood & that no sale shall be made of the trees woods or underwoods thereof or any part thereof in witness whereof both parties have interchangeably set their hands and seals the day and year first within written

Peter Hedgman (Seal)
William M Turner (Seal)
his mark

Signed, Sealed and Delivered in the presence of
John Mauzy **Joseph Delaney** **William Cagi**

The word, granted, in ye 4th line and the word, to consist of 200, in the 25th line & the words, one thousand, in the 30th line & the word, or, in the 36th line being first interlined & allso the word 50£ Sterling & in the 34th line and also the words, and the quitrents of the said land, in the 23rd line being all first interlined."

Recorded with these three leases were three more leases from Peter HEDGMAN to Joseph DELANEY, William CAGE and James FREEMAN. William TURNER (by mark) and Edward TURNER witnessed all three of these leases and they were all acknowledged on 26 May 1746.[20] By 1752 William TURNER was in court bringing suit against Joseph CAGE for trespass.[21] By March of 1754 James FREEMAN had died and in September 1755 Edward TURNER, William TURNER and John BARBY were suing the widow and her new husband, John and Elizabeth WELCH, for counter security in James FREEMAN'S estate.[22]

A man named Stephen MCCORMICK (brother of the John MCCORMICK who witnessed Mary JENNINGS will in 1745 along with William TURNER)[23] was overseer on Peter HEDGMAN'S land in Fauquier (HEDGMAN'S Quarter also called Merry Hill).

Stephen MCCORMICK had a long running court case against James TURNER from 1753 until 1755 when the case was dismissed. Edward TURNER, Jane TURNER, William TURNER and Sarah TURNER were each paid for two days travel to court on the 24 September 1754. These may be the wives of Edward and William TURNER. On the 24 March 1755 they were all paid again, 1 day for each, except three days for William TURNER.[24]

Fauquier County was formed on 1 May 1759 from the western portion of Prince William County. The 1759 Fauquier County Tithables List has been preserved. In the list of Thos. MARSHALL we find:

HEDGMAN'S Quarter	}
Steven MCCORMACK & negroes	} 12 tithables
William TURNER	}
Alexr. TURNER	} 3 tithables
Edwd. TURNER	}
James TURNER	1 tithable[25]

This shows that Steven MCCORMICK was overseer with 11 Negro slaves on Peter HEDGMAN'S Quarter. James TURNER was living in a separate household. William, Alexander and Edward TURNER appear to be living together. None of the TURNERS own slaves. William and Edward should be the two men (or their two sons) who had the 1746 leases from Peter HEDGMAN. Alexander TURNER was the son of Edward and Jean TURNER, born in 1741 and baptized at Overwharton Parish, Stafford County.[26] Edward TURNER was married to Jane GIBSON of Prince William County. She was named in the will of her father, Jacob GIBSON, dated 2 October 1734, "to my daughter Jann TURNER one young mair."[27]

Peter HEDGMAN, who died in 1765, left a will dated 29 November 1764.[28] In this will he left 500 acres of land in Fauquier County to Margaret MCCORMICK, wife of his overseer Stephen MCCORMICK. This included the 400 acres of land that was leased to William and Edward TURNER in 1746. At the time the will was written in 1764 the land was occupied by James and William TURNER (sons of Edward and William respectively).

"Item I Give unto Margaret MCCORMICK, wife of Stephen MCCORMICK, four hundred acres of Land in the County of Fauquier whereon is now two Tenements Occupied by William TURNER and James TURNER, likewise one hundred Acres of Land adjoining the same which will take in the whole or part of what

James GRIMSLY formerly lived on so as to make the whole Lands to her hereby devised a Tract of five hundred Acres."[29]

At May Court 1767 there was a suit brought by Aminadab SEEKRIGHT Plaintiff against Ferdinando DREADNOUGHT Defendant "In Ejectment for one messuage and 200 acres of land with the appurtenances situate lying and being in the Parish of Hamilton and county of Fauquier of the demise of Edward TURNER. On the motion of Stephen MCCORMAC he is admitted Deft. in this suit in the room of the said DREADNOUGHT and thereupon by William ELLZEY his attorney he comes and defends the force and injury when etc. and pleads the general issue and agrees to insist on the title only at Trial."[30]

At the June Court 1768 Aminadab SEEKRIGHT Plaintiff against Stephen MCCORMICK Deft "In Ejectment for one messuage tenement & 200 acres of land with the appurtenances in the Parish of Hamilton in the County of Fauquier of the Demise of Edward TURNER. Discontinued being agreed."[31]

The names being used for the Plaintiff and Defendant seem to be the same as we now use John DOE and Richard ROE. Stephen MCCORMICK, whose wife Margaret had inherited this land, was now trying to eject Edward TURNER from his 200 acres of leased land. The word "demise" can mean either death or "a death or decease occasioning the transfer of an estate." A "messuage" is "a dwelling with its adjacent buildings and lands."[32]

In March of 1767 the petition of Edward TURNER against John KNOX Executor of Peter HEDGMAN was dismissed because the "Sheriff having returned that the Deft is no inhabitant of this county." So possibly Edward TURNER was the man who originally took out the lease for 200 acres from Peter HEDGMAN in 1746, but he had moved out of Fauquier County. This could explain why his son, James TURNER, was occupying the leased land in 1765 at the time of the writing of Peter HEDGMAN'S will. In the November Court of 1769 Edward TURNER was called "an aged witness." At October Court 1776, Edward TURNER was "discharged from paying county levys for the future." This was usually because of age.[33]

Their was no suit for ejectment of William TURNER from his lease. John Meridy TURNER did not seem to have any part in any lawsuits over this land. Stephen MCCORMICK died in 1786 and his wife, Margaret, survived him. He gave her "all of my Estate during her natural life and after her decease to be divided between

Our two children John MACORMICK and Elizabeth Mtjoy MARTIN."[34] There was no record of a will for Margaret MCCORMICK. The MCCORMICKS are remembered for their grandson, Stephen MCCORMICK (1784-1875), who patented a cast-iron mould board plow in 1819.[35]

On the 26 April 1779 John (Meridy) TURNER purchased 150 acres of land for £100 from Reuben and Mary WRIGHT at the Marsh Run, corner to Mrs. ALEXANDER. This was just south of the present town of Bealeton on present US 17. The north end of the plantation was near Marr's Bridge on Marsh Road, now US 17. On the same day Reuben and Mary WRIGHT sold 200 acres to Nicholas WYCOFF described as lying near Marsh Run, Mr. HUNTER, and Rogues Road.[36] Reuben WRIGHT of Fauquier County had patented 422 acres adjacent Col. Charles CARTER, Mr. THORN, Mr. SKINKER and the "Roages Road" on 5 April 1775.[37] "Rogues Road" was another designation for the "Old Carolina Road," portions of which still traverse parts of the county.[38]

In 1775 the population of Fauquier County was about 13,500. About 4,800 of these were slaves owned by about 15 per cent of the white male population, or about 650 persons. At least half of these 650 men owned between one and four slaves.[39] The farmers raised corn to feed themselves and their hogs and cattle. The wife and children tended the vegetable garden. Their only marketable crop was tobacco. John TURNER worked his land with his two sons and his Negroes.

In 1779, John Meridy TURNER, a man in his thirties, was married and had several children. The country was at war with Great Britain, but we found no record of him serving in the Revolution. There was a record for 30 July 1780 of a John TURNER providing supplies (8 pounds of Bacon) for the Revolutionary Army.[40] During the Revolution, the tread of marching feet on the Carolina Road could be heard. In January, 1779, the Saratoga Convention prisoners passed over it on their way to Charlottesville, and two years later "mad" Anthony WAYNE followed with his brigade of the Pennsylvania Line to reinforce LAFAYETTE'S army in the campaign that ended at Yorktown.[41]

The marriage of John Meridy TURNER to Elizabeth was not recorded in Fauquier, but they must have married sometime around 1770. The marriages of their two sons and three daughters were all recorded in Fauquier County. The marriage of Sarah to Lewis BROWN was not recorded. Lewis BROWN was listed in Edward

HUMSTON'S 1787 tax list.[42] John TURNER was in the same list. There were two John TURNERS listed in the Personal Property Tax Books for Fauquier County from 1782 to 1788. In 1788 Willis BROWN was listed in the same household with John TURNER in Edward HUMSTON'S list.[43]

The 1800 Tax List (Charles PICKETT'S List) has:

TURNER, John	1 free male over 16, 5 horses, 2 slaves over 16.
TURNER, Daniel	1 free male over 16, 1 horse
SMITH, Lewis	1 free male over 16, 2 horses.[44]

John TURNER was on the 1810 census with his wife, one son and one daughter (probably his unmarried children, John Meredith and Mary) and seven slaves.[45]

A declaration of war against Great Britain was passed by Congress on 18 June 1812. According to his service record, John Meredith TURNER enlisted at Germantown, Fauquier County, on 25 Aug 1814 (the day after the British attack on Washington D.C.) and was discharged 24 Nov 1814 for a total of three months service. His unit, among others, was positioned for the defense of Baltimore and would have witnessed the British attack on Ft. McHenry in Baltimore harbor on 13 Sep 1814. The Star Spangled Banner was written by Francis Scott KEY during this battle.[46]

Since John Meridy TURNER bought only one piece of land in his lifetime, the best record of his life is his death in 1815. He seems to have lived his whole life in this very small area of Fauquier County, moving from his father's plantation near Remington to his own plantation near Bealeton. That is a distance of about three miles.

Here is a complete copy of his original will:

"In the name of god. Amen, the 16th day of May 1815
I, **John Turner**, of Fauquier County, being in perfect memory, praise be to Almighty god for the same, yet calling to mind the uncertainty of this life, and the certainty of death, I do make and appoint this my last Will and Testament, in form Following. I therefore commit my soul to Almighty god, which gave it, and my body to the earth to be buried after a decent and christian like manner, According to the discretion of my Executors hereafter named, and as touching my worldly Estate, which it hath pleased Almighty god to bless me with, in this life, I give devise and dispose of them in manner and form following (Viz.)

I therefore order that all my Just debts and burial charges be fully paid, and satisfied, before any part thereof is taken out of the hands and possession of my Executors, hereafter named.

First, I give and bequeath unto my beloved wife, **Elizabeth Turner**, all my Real and personal Estate (after all my Just debts are paid) during her natural life, then to be divided in the manner and form following.

I also give To my Son, **Daniel Turner**, one negroe Woman named **Ruth**.

I also give to my Daughter **Elizabeth Oliver** one negroe man named **Leroy**, during her natural life, then to belong to my grandson **John Brown**.

I also give to my Son **John M. Turner** one negroe man named **Lewis**, one feather bed, and one cow & calf.

I also give to my Daughter **Mary H. Turner**, one negroe woman named **Mariah** and her two children, named **Richard & Wilson**, and all the said **Mariah's** future increase and one feather bed, one horse, one cow & calf.

I also give to my Daughter **Hannah Smith**, one negroe woman named **Nancy** & one named **Susannah**, and there future increase to her dureing her natural life, then to be equally divided among all her children.

I also give To my Daughter **Sally Brown** one negroe boy named **Tom**, but to remain with my Daughter **Mary H. Turner** untill demanded.

And lastly all the residue of my real and personal Estate to be sold and the money equally divided among all of my Children, after all of my Just debts are paid.

I hereby appoint my friends **Robert Green**, **Lewis Suddoth**, & **Joseph Morgan**, my Executors of this my last Will and Testament, hereby revoking all other wills made by me. In witness whereof I have hereunto set my hand and seal the day and year above written in the thirty fifth line the words (the residue) was interlined before sighn.

his
John X Turner (Seal)
mark

Sighn Sealed, published, and declared by the above named **John Turner** to be his last will and testament in the presence of us who have hereunto subscribed our names as witnesses in the presence of the testator.
Joseph Boteler
John Suddoth
Cossm B Day

At a Court held for Fauqr. County the 26th day of June 1815 This Will was proved by the oaths of **Joseph Boteler**, **John Suddoth**, and **Cossom B. Day** witnesses thereto & ordered to be Recorded and on the motion of **Robt. Green**, **Lewis Suddoth**, and **Joseph Morgan** the Executors therein named who together with, **John Suddoth**, **Geo. Eastham Jr.** & **Inman Horner** their securities who entered into an ackd. bond in the penalty of four thousand Dollars conditioned as the Law directs a certificate is granted them for obtaining a probate thereof in due form. Teste **Danl. Withers**."[47]

During colonial times, the law in Virginia had been that the wife received her dower (one-third) share in the real estate during her lifetime and the eldest son received two-thirds, and his mother's share upon her death.[48] John TURNER left the whole of his estate to his wife during her life, and then at the time of her death the estate was to be divided (according to his wishes) among all their children.

At June Court 1815 Thomas GREEN, William FRANKLIN, Joseph BOTELER & John SUTHARD [SUDDOTH] or any three of them were sworn to appraise the estate of John TURNER. The inventory was made on 23 August and recorded on the 25 September.[49] The slaves were valued at Laroy $500, Lewis $500, Thomas $500, Nancy $250, Ruth $300, Maria $400, Sucky $400, Richard $150, Wilson $100. The estate, not counting the real estate, was appraised at a total of $3707.75.

The widow, Elizabeth TURNER, was to live out her life on the plantation with the assistance of her slaves and her son, John Meredith TURNER, who stayed with his mother until after her death. In September of 1816, her daughter Mary H. was married to John GARNER by George LEMMON, Episcopal minister. The marriage bond was dated 21 September 1816 and the bondsman was Lewis SUDDOTH, the executor of her father's estate.[50] A prenuptial agreement was signed by John GARNER on the 21 September 1816 stating that he would have no right to the property of Mary TURNER that was to come into her possession at the death of her mother. In this deed he was said to be John GARNER of the County of Hardy. Hardy County is now in West Virginia.[51]

The 1820 census for Fauquier County finds Elizabeth TURNER with ten slaves and what appears to be her son John Meredith TURNER, his wife Harriet and their daughter Elizabeth all living with her.[52]

At the Fauquier Court for 24 January 1825 William BOWER, John B. GIBSON & Aldridge JAMES were sworn to settle the accounts of Joseph MORGAN & Lewis SUDDOTH the Executors of John TURNER. They reported that Elizabeth TURNER had accepted the appraisal of her husband's personal estate as $3,707.75 on the 29 April 1824. This was recorded on the 25 April 1825.[53]

So it would be sometime after this date of 29 April 1824 and before the appraisal of the estate made on 26 August 1828 that Elizabeth TURNER died. On that date John EUSTACE, William HANSBOROUGH, George DUFF & John SUDDOTH were sworn to appraise the estate again. At this appraisal the slaves were not included (since they were given to the children in the will), but the 152 acres of Land was appraised at $2.25 per acre for a total of $342.00. The total estate was then valued at $616.70.[54]

A sale of the estate was held on 4 September 1828 and this was recorded on 23 March 1829 for a total of $624.07.[55] This was quite close to the valuation placed on the estate by the appraisers. This sale shows that the family had gathered at the old home place for the final sale. Even though Daniel TURNER and Hannah SMITH had already moved on to Shenandoah County, Daniel was back for the sale. Hannah had sent her son Alexander SMITH to represent her. Mary GARNER, Samuel OLIVER and John TURNER were also at the sale. Nothing was said about whether they received the slaves at this time or if they were also sold. The proceeds were divided and that was the end of this TURNER family in Fauquier County, Virginia. It had been eighty-two years since William, Edward, and James TURNER took out their leases for three lives.

Since it is interesting to see what the worldly estate of our ancestor consisted of, we will transcribe the full sale list:

"A List of the sales of the Estate of John Turner decd sold 4th of Sept. 1828.

1 pine press	**Samuel Oliver**	$0.70
1 pine Cupboard	**John Turner**	1.00
1 desk	**John Turner**	1.00
1 tea table and tea board	**Alexander Smith**	1.75
1 pine table & 3 tea canisters	**John Turner**	0.40
5 pewter plates & 1 dish	**John Turner**	2.10
2 basins, 2 old tin pans and 1 spoon	**John Turner**	0.95
1 bed, bedstead and furniture	**Mary M. Garner**	2.95
1 bed, bedstead and furniture	**John Turner**	6.10
1 bed and furniture	**Wm. Berryman**	2.10
1 pine chest	**Mary M. Garner**	1.10
1 flax wheel	**Wm. Wright**	1.15
1 flax wheel	**William Oliver**	0.55
1 Cotton wheel	**William Oliver**	0.25
1 Cotton wheel	**John Taylor**	0.05
3 Chairs	**William Oliver**	0.35
1 slaie	**John Turner**	0.40
1 slaie	**John Turner**	0.65
1 slaie	**James Arrowsmith**	0.80
1 Loom & Harness	**John Turner**	1.00
1 stone pot & pitcher	**John Turner**	0.65
2 small stone pots	**Wm. Berryman**	0.35
4 old tubs	**Wm. Berryman**	0.80
2 potracks & old tongs	**John Turner**	0.55
1 spice mortar & flesh forks	**Alexander Smith**	1.05
2 dutch ovens	**John Turner**	0.35
1 pair of wedges	**Wm. Berryman**	0.75
2 pots & pot hooks	**John Turner**	1.65
2 axes	**John Turner**	1.20
4 old hoes	**Thomas Evans**	0.80
1 large plough, swingletree & Clivis iron	**James Bustle**	0.60
1 large plough, swingletree & Clivis iron	**John Turner**	0.65
1 shovel plough	**William Baker**	0.70
3 pair of Cards	**Allen Bustle**	0.75
1 Hackle	**George Smallwood**	0.20
1 sythe & cradle	**John Turner**	1.25
1 sythe & cradle	**Charles Cook**	1.15
1 Harrow	**Samuel Puckett**	0.80
1 walnut table	**William Oliver**	2.50
1 waggon & hind gear	**John Turner**	44.25

2 bridles and Old gear	**Alexander D. Kelly**	1.80
old irons in barrel	**Silas West**	0.50
1 brown bay mare	**Daniel Turner**	27.50
1 bay mare	**John Kenny**	6.50
1 black horse	**John Turner**	27.00
1 iron grey mare 3 years old	**Daniel Turner**	38.50
1 iron Grey Colt	**Enock Jameson**	17.25
1 white face heifer red	**Solas West**	6.25
1 spotted barrow	**Burrel Rector**	3.25
1 red spotted Sow	**Wm. Berryman**	2.50
1 sandy Coloured sow	**Burrel Rector**	1.75
1 white & black sow	**Burrel Rector**	1.75
3 spotted shoats	**Burrel Rector**	4.00
1 rye shock	**John Suddoth**	0.45
1 hay stack	**Landon Allen**	3.00
1st 5 barrels of corn $1:75 pr barrel	**Wm. Wyckoff**	8.75
2nd 5 barrels of Do $1:75 pr Do	**Wm. Wyckoff**	8.75
3rd 5 barrels of Do $1:75 pr Do	**Wm. Wyckoff**	8.50
1st 6 sheep	**Joseph Rector**	6.05
2nd 7 sheep	**John Taylor**	6.20
Fodder & corn shucks	**Wm. Wyckoff**	4.55
Wool	**Joseph Morgan**	0.27
spun yarn	**Wm. Preston**	2.52
short corn $3:20=1/2 bushels of corn 52cts	**John Turner**	3.72
152 acres of Land $2:31 pr acre	**Carola G. A. Jennings**	351.12
		$624.07

At a Court held for Fauquier County 23d March 1829
This account of sales was returned & ordered to be recorded.
test **John A. W. Smith** Clk."

The sale of the land was executed in a deed dated 17 October 1828 between Carola G. A. JENNINGS & Mary his wife to Lewis SUDDOTH for $351.12 paid by Lewis SUDDOTH, confirming unto Lewis SUDDOTH one certain tract being "that part of the tract of land on which John TURNER resided at the time of his death & of which he died possessed & on which the dwelling house & other houses stand."[56]

Another deed was recorded on the same date, 31 August 1829, between Carola G. A. JENNINGS & Mary his wife for $351 from

Joseph MORGAN for one certain parcel of land lying on the waters of Marsh Run in Fauquier being a part of the tract of land owned by John TURNER decd. at the time of his death & bounded as follows "Beginning at a large Spanish oak standing at the junction of North Marsh & Elk Marsh runs and running thence to John SUDDOTH and Lewis SUDDOTH to a dead maple standing near the head of the Big Beaver dam thence up the meanders of the Marsh Run to the beginning."[57] It appears that JENNINGS was an intermediary so that the executors of John TURNER could buy his land.

An account of the Executors was made on 26 October 1829 showing they had receipts of $505.90½ which (minus what they had spent) left a total balance of $289.98. "The estate of Jno. TURNER decd. in account current with Joseph MORGAN and Lewis SUDDOTH Exors.

1828 Dr.	
To 20 yds linen @ 1/- for the negroes	3.33⅓
" 33# Bacon @ 7¢ for family	2.97
" cash paid Jos. G. DUNLANY for coffin	5.00
" cash paid Elijah WRIGHT'S account	1.75
" cash paid fee bill	2.82
" 2 gallons whiskey at the burial & 8½ gals. do. at the sale at 50¢	5.25
" cash paid Samuel ESKRIDGE for crying sale	3.50
" cash paid for copy of sale	0.70
" cash paid John NEALE pr receipt	9.00
" cash paid for copy of will	0.70
" cash paid Joseph MORGAN'S Blacksmith accot.	4.11
" cash paid 2 chain carriers per receipt	1.00
" cash paid John TURNER'S afc for corn	8.00
" cash paid for a copy of Inventory	0.70
" cash paid for surveying land - Chs. MORGAN	1.50
" Joseph MORGAN'S acct as pr. clks mdm.	76.23
" fee Bil 1828	0.88
" Tax paid for 1828	5.89
" expences of Geo EASTHAM & Wm. THOMPSON} commissioners one day each at 1.00 }	2.00
" commission on 505.90½ cents @ 10 pr.cent	50.59
" amount allowed for records	10.00
To Balance account	289.98
	$505.90½

4 Sep 1829 Cr.	
By account of sales this day due	448.45½

By wheat sold 47 45/00 Bushl.	41.54
By cash received of W. A. BOTELER	12.41
By cash of John EUSTACE	3.50
	$505.90½

4 Sep 1929	
By Balance due the estate	$289.98

Fauquier County, to wit.

Pursuant to the order of Fauquier County Court bearing date the 26th October 1829, we have examined & settled the acct. of Lewis SUDDUTH & Joseph MORGAN Exors. of John TURNER decd. & settled the same as above stated.

Wm. THOMPSON
Geo. EASTHAM

At a court held for Fauquier County on the 22nd day of March 1830 This account and report was returned and ordered to lie 60 days for exceptions.
And at a court held for said county on the 24th day of May 1830 The same was confirmed & ordered to be recorded.

Teste
Jno. AROSMITH Clk."[58]

The final account of the Executors was made on the 15 Nov 1830. The estate had a balance of $465.54. The six heirs were paid $68.72½ each. They were named as "Lewis BROWN who intermarried Sarah TURNER, John M. TURNER, Lewis SMITH who intermarried with Hannah TURNER per Saml. PERRYS Recpt., Saml. PERRY attorney for Daniel TURNER, Saml. OLIVER who intermarried with Eliza TURNER, Mary H. GARNER." The account was recorded on 29 July 1834.[59]

From this final account in 1830 it appears that all of the children were still living in Fauquier County, except for Daniel TURNER and Hannah SMITH of Shenandoah County who were represented by power of attorney. The attorney was Samuel PERRY who had married Elizabeth McCarty SMITH(23), 25 November 1824, in Fauquier, Virginia. He was in the 1830 Shenandoah County census.

MAP OF VIRGINIA COUNTIES

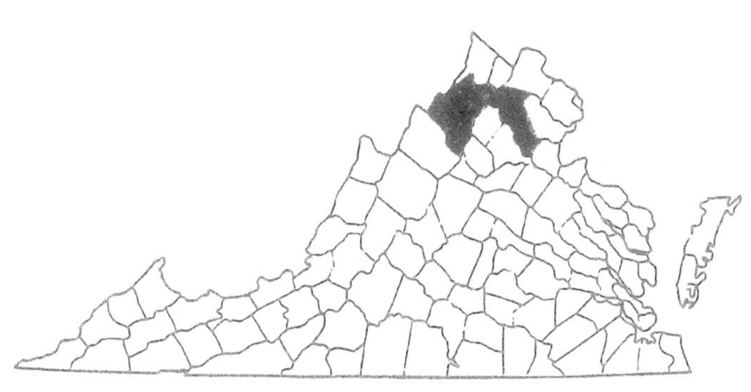

SHENANDOAH AND FAUQUIER COUNTIES IN 1830

The first English immigrants arrived in Virginia in 1607. Virginia became a royal colony in 1624 and continued in that form until it became an independent Commonwealth in 1776. The County of Prince William was formed in 1730 out of King George and Stafford Counties. Fauquier County was formed from Prince William in 1759. Frederick County was formed from Orange and Augusta Counties in 1738 to 1743. Shenandoah was formed from Frederick County in 1772 and at that time included parts of the present day Counties of Page and Warren.

THE TURNER FAMILIES LIVED IN FAUQUIER AND SHENANDOAH COUNTIES

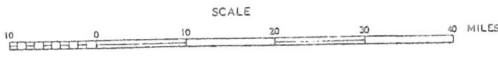

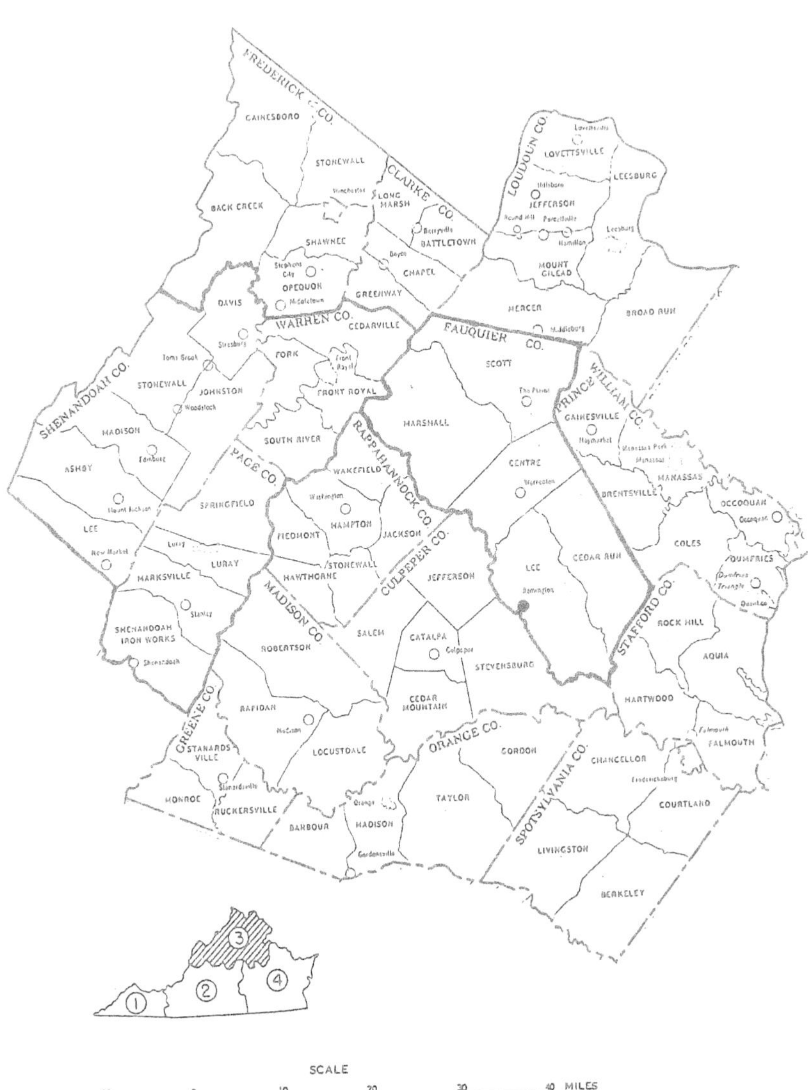

FAUQUIER COUNTY VIRGINIA

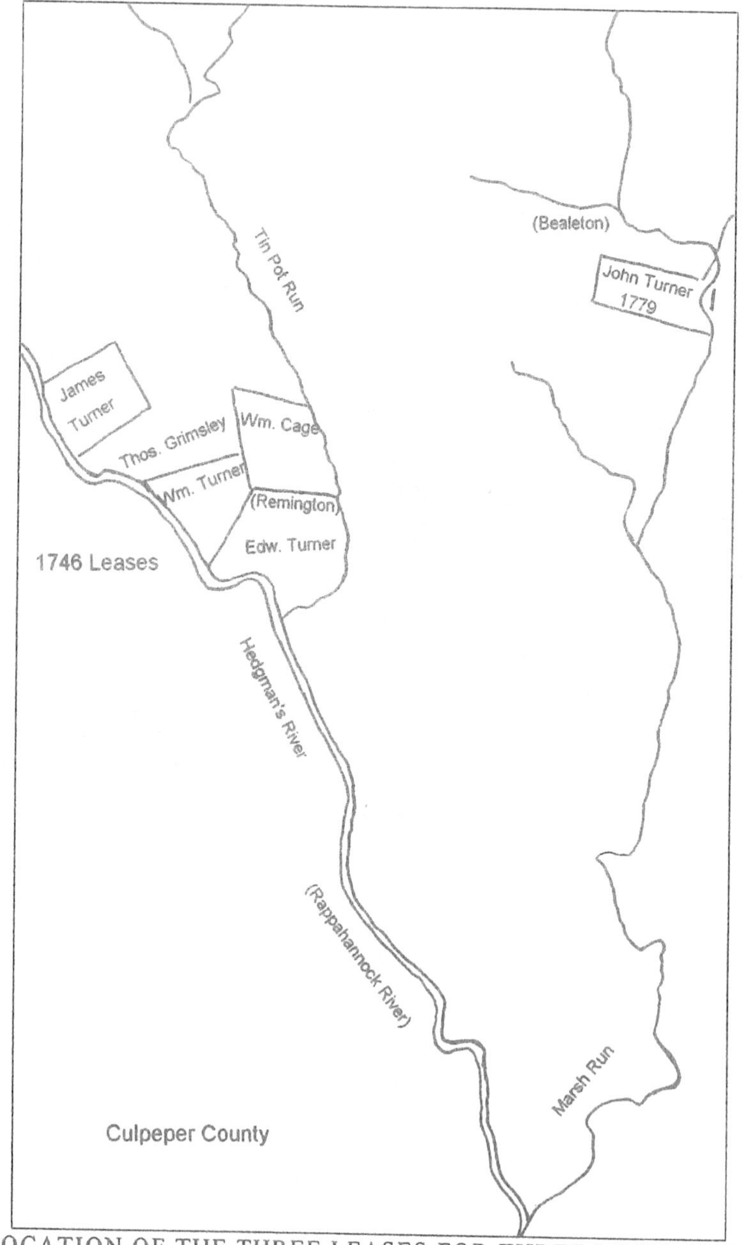

LOCATION OF THE THREE LEASES FOR THREE LIVES AND THE LAND PURCHASE OF JOHN MERIDY TURNER IN 1779

FIRST GENERATION

1. **John Meridy[1] TURNER**, son of William TURNER. Born, before 1747, probably in Prince William, VA. Died, Jun 1815, in Fauquier, VA.[60]

He married Elizabeth [UNKNOWN], circa 1770, in Fauquier, VA. Died, 1828, in Fauquier, VA.[61] Children:

2 i. Sarah (Sally)[2] TURNER, Born 1770, in Fauquier, VA. She married Lewis BROWN in Fauquier, VA. A Lewis BROWN is on the 1787 tax list in Edward HUMSTON'S district. In 1794 Lewis BROWN was named as a chain carrier on a survey of a plot of land on Marsh Road and Marsh Run in a trespass dispute.[62] He collected his wife's share of her father's estate in 1830 and there is a Lewis BROWN on the 1830 Fauquier, VA census.

\+ 3 ii. Elizabeth TURNER.

\+ 4 iii. Daniel Meridy TURNER.

\+ 5 iv. Hannah TURNER.

6 v. Mary H. TURNER. Born before 1784, in Fauquier, VA. She married John GARNER of Hardy County, VA, Sep 1816 in Fauquier, VA. She collected her share of her father's estate in 1830.

\+ 7 vi. John Meredith TURNER.

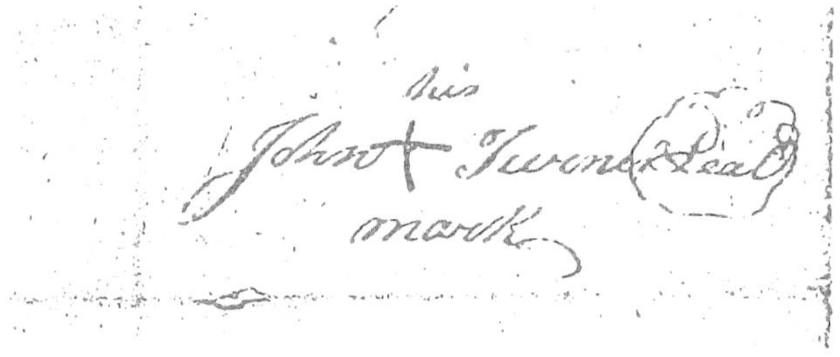

JOHN TURNER'S MARK FROM HIS WILL WRITTEN IN 1815.

NOTES: CHAPTER 1 - FIRST GENERATION

---

[1]Nancy Chappelear and John K. Gott, *Early Fauquier County, Virginia, Marriage Bonds, 1759-1854* (Washington, DC, 1965), p. 1.

[2] Carol McGinnis, *Virginia Genealogy: Sources & Resources* (Baltimore: Genealogical Publishing Co., 1993), p. 91.

[3] Ibid., pp. 193-194.

[4] "Register of St. Stephens Parish, Northumberland Co., Virginia" [A copy of the original alphabetized at a later date. Original is lost.], Beverley Fleet, *Virginia Colonial Abstracts* (Baltimore: Genealogical Publishing Co., 1961) 3:87 (94), 89 (98).

[5] Ibid., 3:8 (20N), 106 (123).

[6] John Frederick Dorman, *Westmoreland County, Virginia: Order Book 1690-1698*, 3 vols. (Washington, DC, 1962-1964), p. 150a.

[7] John Frederick Dorman, *Westmoreland County, Virginia, Deeds, Patents, Etc., 1665-1667*, 4 vols. (Washington, DC, 1973-1974), p. 41.

[8] John Frederick Dorman, *Westmoreland County, Virginia Deeds and Wills No. 6, 1716-1720* (Washington, DC, 1989), p. 27.

[9] James F. Lewis and J. Motley Booker, *Northumberland County, Virginia, Wills and Administrations*, 4 vols. (Kilmarnock, VA: 1964-1967) 4:113.

[10] Ruth Ritchie and Sudie Rucker Wood, *Garner-Keene Families of Northern Neck, Virginia* (Charlottesville?, VA: 1952), p. 12.

[11] Ibid., p. 17 (Westmoreland Deed and Will Book 8:320).

[12] Ibid., p. 23 (Westmoreland Deed and Will Book 10:119).

[13] David Wolfe Eaton, *Historical Atlas of Westmoreland County, Virginia* (Richmond, VA: Dietz Press, 1942), p. 10.

[14] Jane A. Lion, "A List of Voters in the 1741 Burgess Election from Westmoreland County, Virginia," *The Virginia Genealogist* (1981), 25:275-277.

[15] George H. S. King, *King George County, Virginia, Will Book A-1, 1721-1752, and Miscellaneous Notes* (Fredericksburg, VA: 1978), p. 159.

[16] H. C. Groome, *Fauquier During the Proprietorship* (Richmond: 1927, Baltimore: Regional Publishing Company, reprint 1969), pp. 84-85.

[17] Ibid.

[18] Prince William County, Virginia Deeds, I:68, 70, 74. Film #33106.

[19] Martin, *Martin Family History*, p. 2.

[20] Prince William County, Virginia Deeds, I:64, 66, 72. Film #33106.

---

[21] Prince William County, Virginia Minute Book (1752-1753), p. 35.

[22] Prince William County, Virginia Order Book (1754-1755), pp. 18, 315.

[23] Their father was Neal MCCORMICK. King George County Will Book A:163 dated 25 Sep 1736.

[24] Prince William County Order Book (1754-1755), pp. 143, 190.

[25] 1759 Fauquier County, Virginia Tithables. Thos. Marshall's List p.4 col.1 [accn #24569 Virginia State Archives]

[26] George H. S. King, ***The Register of Overwharton Parish, Stafford County, Virginia, 1723-1758*** ... (Fredericksburg, VA: 1961), p. 120.

[27] John Frederick Dorman, ***Prince William County, Virginia Will Book C 1734-1744*** (Washington, DC: 1956), p. 7 (35).

[28] George Harrison Sanford King, "Notes From the Journal of John Mercer, Esquire, (1704/5-1768) of Marlborough, Stafford County, Virginia," ***The Virginia Genealogist*** (1960), 4:152.

[29] Stafford County, Virginia Will Book, O:488.

[30] Fauquier County Minute Book (1764-1768), p. 274. Film #31613.

[31] Fauquier County Minute Book (1764-1768), p. 375. Film #31613.

[32] ***Random House Webster's College Dictionary*** (New York: Random House, 1991), pp. 360, 850.

[33] Fauquier County Minute Books, (1764-1768), p. 251. Film #31613; (1768-1773), p. 156; (1773-1780), p. 269. Film #31614

[34] Fauquier County, Virginia Wills, Book 2:89-90.

[35] T. Triplett Russell and John K. Gott, ***Fauquier County In the Revolution*** (Warrenton, VA: Fauquier County American Bicentennial Commission, 1976), p. 39; ***Dictionary of American Biography*** (1933), 6:614.

[36] Fauquier County, Virginia Deeds, 7:61-65.

[37] Gertrude E. Gray, ***Virginia Northern Neck Land Grants, Volume II, 1742-1775*** (Baltimore: Genealogical Publishing Co., 1988), p. 105.

[38] Groome, ***Fauquier During the Proprietorship***, p. 193; Martin, ***Martin Family History***, p. 3.

[39] Russell and Gott, ***Fauquier County In the Revolution***, p. 1.

[40] Virginia Public Service Claims, Fauquier County. Film #029810.

[41] Groome, ***Fauquier During the Proprietorship***, p. 194.

[42] Netti Schreiner-Yantis and Florene Speakman Love, ***The 1787 Census of Virginia***, 3 vols. (Springfield, VA.: Genealogical Books in Print, 1987), I:277.

[43] Fauquier County, Virginia, Personal Property Tax Books 1782-1788, Virginia State Archives, Microfilm Reel 123.

[44] "1800 Tax List," ***The Virginia Genealogist*** (1977), 21:186.

[45] 1810 Fauquier County, Virginia, Census, p. 416.

[46] War of 1812 Records, Service Index, 36th Regt (Renno's) Virginia Militia, John TURNER, Pvt., National Archives; Stuart Lee Butler, *A Guide to Virginia Militia Units in the War of 1812* (Athens, GA: Iberian Pub. Co., 1988), pp. 82-83, 180.

[47] Fauquier County Wills, Book 6:123.

[48] McGinnis, *Virginia Genealogy*, p. 106.

[49] Fauquier County Wills, Book 6:148.

[50] John K. Gott, *Fauquier County, Virginia Marriage Bonds: 1759-1854 and Marriage Returns: 1785-1848* (Bowie, MD: Heritage Books, 1989), p. 73.

[51] Fauquier County Deeds, 21:80.

[52] 1820 Fauquier County, Virginia, Census, p. 90A.

[53] Fauquier County Wills, Book 9:209.

[54] Fauquier County Wills, Book 10:463.

[55] Fauquier County Wills, Book 10:464.

[56] Fauquier County Deeds, 30:422.

[57] Fauquier County Deeds, 30:521.

[58] Fauquier County Wills, Book 11:208-209.

[59] Fauquier County Wills, Book 13:352.

[60] Fauquier County Wills, Book 6:123.

[61] She was alive 29 April 1824 when the executor's account was presented to court, but deceased by 4 Sept. 1828 when the estate sale for John TURNER was held.

[62] Fauquier County Misc. Court Records, 1759-1882, p. 87. Film #31610.

CHAPTER 2

THE SECOND GENERATION

The children of John Meridy TURNER(1) left their old home in Fauquier County, Virginia. Daniel Meridy TURNER(4) married Mary SMITH and Lewis SMITH married Hannah TURNER(5) in 1796 in Fauquier. Shortly after their marriages, they settled over the mountains in Shenandoah County, Virginia in what is now Page County, Virginia, near Compton, just north of Luray. This was about 50 miles from their home in Fauquier County.

Sometime after the 1830 census the four children of John Meridy TURNER (that we can trace) had all left Virginia. The free state of Ohio was to be their next home. The son of Lewis and Hannah SMITH, John M. T. SMITH(21), was in Hamilton County, Ohio as early as 1829 when a daughter was born there and they were on the 1830 census. Samuel and Elizabeth PERRY(23) were in Delaware County, Ohio sometime between 1831 and 1840. The NORTH-CRAFTS(24) were in Ohio in 1836. Alexander SMITH(25) and his family were in Ohio by 1833. Daniel Meridy TURNER'S(4) family had a short stopover in Ohio with a child born there about 1835. Maria Louisa TURNER(19) married Michael MILLER in Coshocton County, Ohio in 1838. For most of the SMITH and Daniel TURNER family it was a short stay in Ohio as they were in Missouri by 1838.

Study of the 1850 census returns pinpoint quite accurately when the families left Virginia for Ohio. The 1850 census was the first census to list the birthplaces of the family members. From this we can verify that the families of John Meredith and Harriet COOKE TURNER(7) and Samuel and Elizabeth TURNER OLIVER(3) arrived in Ohio sometime between 1831 and 1835. They located in southeast Licking County, near the Muskingum County border.

They could not bring their slaves to Ohio. Ohio was a free state. They would no longer be raising tobacco as a cash crop. Principal agricultural products in Licking County, Ohio were wheat, corn, oats, barley, buckwheat, sorghum and potatoes.[1]

The two families lived in Franklin Township. Samuel OLIVER bought property in section 11 in March of 1839.[2] John Meredith TURNER lived just a few miles north in Section 1. He remained in

Franklin Township until 1850 when he purchased 100 acres in Perry Township. He held this land only a short time before selling it on 22 September 1851 when all of the families were preparing to move west to Missouri.[3] During the Ohio stay of almost twenty years, many of the younger generation married.

The COOKE family also moved to Licking County. John Meredith TURNER and Samuel OLIVER are on the 1840 Franklin Township, Licking County census, along with Wesley COOKE, the brother of Harriet COOKE TURNER. Wesley COOKE probably arrived in Ohio between 1836 and 1839. He had married Nancy Anne EDWARDS about 1832 in Culpeper, VA. They had seven children born in VA and OH. John Wesley COOKE died 26 December 1846 and was buried at the Pleasant Hill Cemetery in Perry Township. The 1850 census of Perry Township, Licking County, Ohio, shows that the widow of Wesley, Nancy COOK, and John TURNER were living very near to each other.[4]

It is a possibility that the father of Harriet COOKE TURNER also came to Ohio. There is a man age 60 to 70 living with the TURNER family on the 1840 census. Charles COOKE (father of Harriet COOKE) was on the Personal Property Tax Lists for Fauquier County from 1798 to 1800 and 1821 to 1825. He was on the Land Tax Lists from 1816 to 1837. He was on the Personal Property Tax Lists for Culpeper County from 1824 to 1835. This seems to indicate that he would have left Virginia about the same time as his son, Wesley COOKE. In the 1831 Culpeper tax list Charles COOKE & Sons are listed. In 1833 Charles and Marshall COOKE were living together and in 1835 Charles, Marshall and Westley COOKE were living together. We assume then that Marshall is also the son of Charles COOKE and he is living alone on the 1838 Culpeper County taxlist.[5]

Of the four children of Charles COOKE that we can identify, three came to Ohio: John Wesley COOKE, Harriet COOKE TURNER(7), and Anne COOKE BROWN(8).

Of the four children of John Meridy TURNER only one, Elizabeth TURNER BROWN OLIVER(3) died in Ohio. The other three families moved on to Missouri. It is here that they were buried. The very large extended family of John Meredith TURNER came to Harrison Township, Scotland County, Missouri in 1851. The clan was clustered near the towns of Arbela and Etna. They rejoined the families of Daniel TURNER and Lewis SMITH who had settled in northeast Missouri as early as 1836 and after only a short stopover in Ohio.

MAP OF OHIO

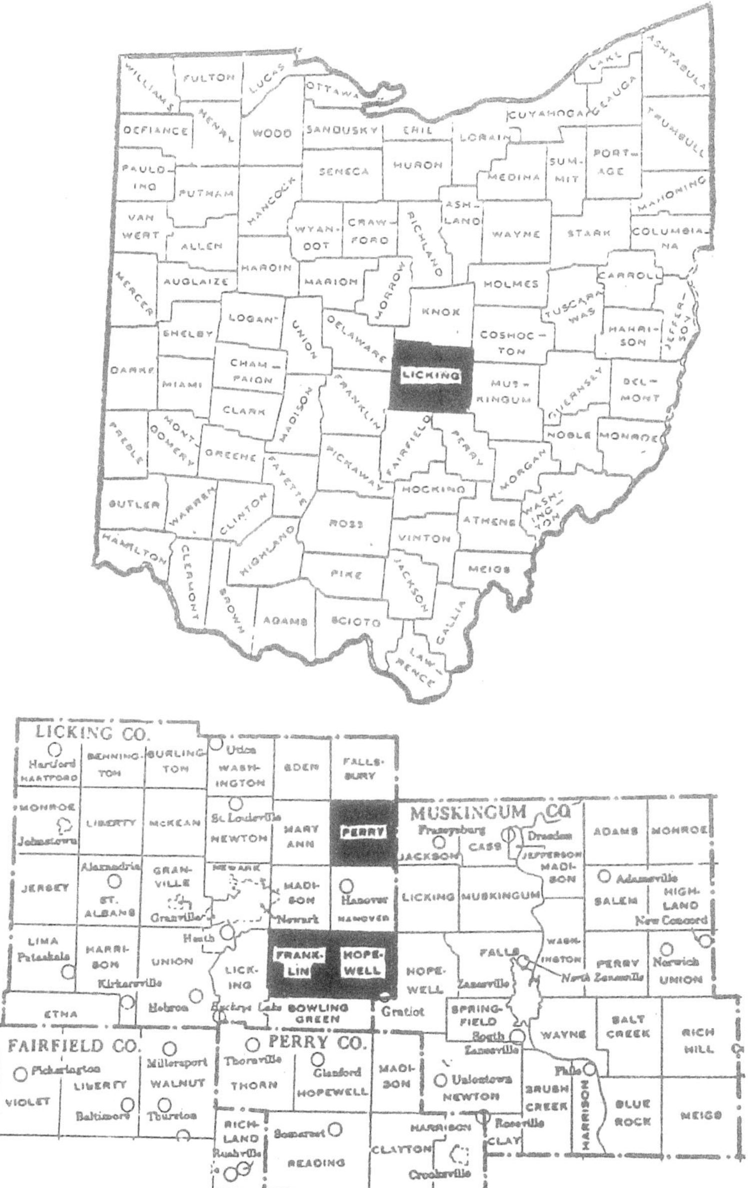

LICKING AND MUSKINGUM COUNTIES

OHIO RECORDS

LICKING CO., OHIO DEEDS
Deed GG-476, John & Elizabeth HART to Samuel OLIVER, Franklin Township, Range 11, Township 1, Section 11, 15 Oct 1838, March 1839.
Deed 60-424, Geo. HAHN to John TURNER, Perry Township, Range 10, Township 3, Lot 5 of the SE quarter, 100 acres, 23 Feb 1850.
Deed 60-425, John TURNER to Thom. N. LEGGIT, the above land, 22 Sep 1851.

1840 U. S. CENSUS for OHIO.
Westley COOK, p. 218 Franklin, Licking, Co.
John TURNER, p. 219 Franklin, Licking, Co.
Samuel OLIVER, p. 219 Franklin, Licking, Co.
Wm. OLIVER, p. 219 Franklin, Licking, Co.
William MARTIN, p. 230 Hopewell, Licking, Co.
John M. BROWN, p. 292 Hopewell, Muskingum, Co.
Levi PRIOR, p. 250 Jackson, Muskingum, Co.

1850 U. S. CENSUS for OHIO.
Peter LIVINGSTON, p. 356 Perry, Licking, Co.
John M. TURNER, p. 363 Perry, Licking, Co.
Nancy COOK, p. 363 Perry, Licking, Co.
David TROUT, p. 243 Bennington, Licking, Co.
William MARTIN, p. 477 Hopewell, Licking, Co.
Samuel MARTIN, p. 80 Hopewell, Muskingum, Co.
Wm. W. MARTIN, p. 81 Hopewell, Muskingum, Co.
Michael CROSS, p. 92 Hopewell, Muskingum, Co.
Levi PRIOR, p. 330 Jackson, Muskingum, Co.

1860 U. S. CENSUS for OHIO.
Peter LIVINGSTON, p. 443 Hopewell, Licking, Co.

1870 U. S. CENSUS for OHIO.
Peter LIVINGSTON, p. 17 Hopewell, Licking, Co.

1880 U. S. CENSUS for OHIO.
Peter LIVINGSTON, p. 12 Perry, Licking, Co.

SECOND GENERATION

3. Elizabeth^2 TURNER (John Meridy, 1). Born, 1771, in Fauquier, VA. Died, 5 Oct 1839, in Gratiot, Licking, OH, buried at the Poplar Fork Cemetery, age 78, as wife of Samuel OLIVER.[6]

She married, first, Willis BROWN, 1 Oct 1791, in Fauquier, VA.[7] He died, before 1806, in Fauquier, VA. Willis BROWN witnessed the statement of John TURNER on the marriage bond of Lewis SMITH and Hannah TURNER in 1796 and was a bondsman for the marriage bond of John OLIVER and Patty WILSON 28 Jan 1797.[8] Children:

8 i. John Meredith BROWN^3. Born, 1792, in Fauquier, VA. He married Anne COOKE, daughter of Charles COOKE and Mary LEGG, 31 Jul 1818, in Fauquier, VA.[9] She was the sister of Wesley COOKE and Harriet COOKE who married John Meredith TURNER(7) in 1817.

9 ii Elizabeth W. BROWN. Born, 1796, in Fauquier, VA. Died, 1870, in Parke, IN, near Catlin, age 74. She married William MARTIN, 26 Sep 1814, in Fauquier, VA. On the same day William MARTIN was named as her guardian with John TURNER as Security. William MARTIN was born, 1792, in VA. Died, 1863, in Parke, IN, age 71.[10]

10 iii. Molly BROWN. Born, 1801, in Fauquier, VA. Meredith ESKRIDGE was her guardian 27 Dec 1819.[11]

She married, second, Samuel OLIVER, 27 Feb 1807, in Fauquier, VA. There is some conflicting information given in the Fauquier marriage bonds. Samuel OLIVER and Elizabeth BROWN, daughter of John, were married 31 Dec 1793 and Simon OLIVER and Elizabeth BROWN, widow of Willis, were married 27 Feb 1807.[12] Samuel OLIVER was on the 1810, 1820 and 1830 census of Fauquier County.[13] He was age 60-70 with one male and one female 20-30 on the 1840 census in Franklin, Licking, Ohio. There is a William OLIVER next to him age 30-40 who may be his son.[14] Died, 27 Feb 1846, in Gratiot, Licking, OH, buried at the Poplar Fork Cemetery, age 75. The cemetery was affiliated with the Primitive Baptist Church until 1925.[15] Children:

	11	iv.	Sarah D. OLIVER. Born, 1809, in VA. Died, 13 Mar 1851, in Gratiot, Licking, OH, age 42. Buried at the Poplar Fork Cemetery.
	12	v.	Samuel L. OLIVER. Born, 27 Aug 1810, in VA. Died, 4 Mar 1893, in Parke, IN, age 82. He married Frances [UNKNOWN], before 1845, in Licking, OH.

4. **Daniel Meridy^2 TURNER** (John Meridy, 1). Born, before 1775, in Fauquier, VA. Died, before 1840, in Clark, MO.

He married Mary SMITH, daughter of Hannah SMITH, 15 Mar 1796, in Fauquier, VA.[16] Born, 1776, in VA. Died, after 1840, in Clark, MO.

In 1795 he signed a petition for the division of Fauquier County into two counties as Daniel Meridy TURNER.[17] He was found on the 1830 census of Shenandoah Co., VA, but not on the 1840 census of Clark Co., MO where his wife was probably living with her son Alexander TURNER. Children:[18]

+	13	i.	William H. TURNER^3.
	14	ii.	Elizabeth TURNER. Born, 1804, in Shenandoah, VA. She married Lewis MILLER, 10 Apr 1826, in Shenandoah, VA.[19]
+	15	iii.	Ann H. (Nancy) TURNER.
+	16	iv.	Alexander S. TURNER.
	17	v.	Sarah TURNER. Born, 1812, in Shenandoah, VA. She married Simon MCFARLAND, 27 Mar 1833, in Shenandoah, VA.[20]
+	18	vi.	Lewis TURNER.
+	19	vii.	Maria Louisa TURNER.
+	20	viii.	James Daniel TURNER.

5. **Hannah^2 TURNER** (John Meridy, 1). Born, 1780, in Fauquier, VA. Died, before 1860, in Scotland, MO.

She married Lewis SMITH, 2 Feb 1796, in Fauquier, VA.[21] Born, 1771, in VA. The will of John SMITH of Hamilton Parish, dated 3 Sep 1776, proved 24 Mar 1777, was attached to the front of Will Book No. 1 of Fauquier County. It names his sister Mary MANRONY, sister Hannah SMITH and her son Lewis SMITH, mother Jane SMITH. They were given land in Dunmore County and a tract in Hamilton Parish where his mother was living was given to his mother during her life and then to be equally divided between Hannah and Lewis.

The estate of Alexander SMITH had been appraised in 1761. Jane SMITH was administrator in 1766.[22] Jane SMITH was named as guardian of her child, Hannah in 1766. Harman SPILMAN was guardian of Jane SMITH in 1766 and Jane SMITH and John SNELLING were named as guardians of Mary SMITH in 1772. Lewis SMITH, orphan of John SMITH, chose Mary SMITH his guardian in 1784. This makes it appear that his mother Hannah SMITH had married a John SMITH.[23]

There was also a marriage record for Lewis SMITH and Ruth DAVIS 21 April 1798, so it was unclear which Lewis SMITH was the son of Hannah SMITH. However, in the marriage bonds, Mary SMITH, daughter of Hannah SMITH, married Daniel TURNER(4) in 1796. On the 21 October 1803 Joseph BLACKWELL & his wife Mary sold to Lewis SMITH a tract on Deep Run being part of a larger tract near Frogs Road, 100 acres for 100£.[24]

Lewis SMITH was then found on the 1810 to 1840 Shenandoah, VA census records. Hannah TURNER SMITH was named in her father's will in 1815 and her husband received her portion of her father's estate in 1830. Children:[25]

21 i. John Meredith Turner SMITH[3]. Born, 11 Aug 1797, in Fauquier, VA. Died, 1 Nov 1883, in Scotland, MO, age 86. He married Alcinda LEHEW. Born, 23 Dec 1807, in VA. Died, 13 Feb 1888, in Scotland, MO, age 80. Both were buried in the Memphis Cemetery. They were in Whitewater, Hamilton, OH on the 1830 census along with a Spencer LEHEW.[26] "John Meredith Turner SMITH settled in Missouri during the year 1842. A group of citizens of Scotland Co. who had resided in the county for a period of about twenty-five years, were called to assemble at the Fairground on Sept. 28, 1871 and organized an Old Settlers' Assoc. Listed on the roll was J. M. T. SMITH from Virginia, age seventy-four years."[27]

22 ii. William Hill SMITH. Born, 1800, in Fauquier, VA. He married, first, Sarah MCFARLAND, daughter of Obediah MCFARLAND and Fany MCKAY, 14 Sep 1821, in Shenandoah, VA.[28] He

married, second, Sallie HERSEY CREIGER.

23 iii. Elizabeth McCarty SMITH. Born, 9 Jun 1801, in Fauquier, VA. Died, 22 Jan 1884, in Audrain, MO, age 82. She married Samuel PERRY, 25 Nov 1824, in Fauquier, VA. The bondsman was John TURNER(7).[29] Born, 11 Apr 1800. Died 2 May 1841, in Delaware, OH near Centervillage, age 41. They were in Shenandoah, VA in 1830.

24 iv. Ann H. "Nancy Ann" SMITH. Born, 16 Apr 1805, in Fauquier, VA. Died, 22 Dec 1881, in Arbela, Scotland, MO, age 76. She married William F. NORTHCRAFT, 26 Feb 1829, in Shenandoah, VA.[30]

25 v. Alexander SMITH. Born, 5 Apr 1807, in Fauquier, VA. Died, 10 May 1889, in Scotland, MO, age 82. Buried in the SMITH Family Cemetery near Arbela, MO. He married Mary E. HERSEY in OH. Born, 10 Oct 1813. Died, 6 Jul 1847, age 33.

26 vi. Daniel Madison SMITH. Born, 1810, in Shenandoah, VA. Died, Aug 1852, in Scotland, MO, age 42.

27 vii. Lewis Turner J. SMITH. Born, 14 May 1815, in Shenandoah, VA. Died, 5 Dec 1890, in Milbayou, Arkansas, AR, age 75. He married Martha ANDERSON, daughter of Hosea ANDERSON and Clarinda ALLINGTON, 13 Feb 1840, in Clark, MO. Born, 1824, OH. Died, 11 Feb 1866, Scotland, MO, age 42.

28 viii. Zerilda Jane SMITH. Born, 1818, in Shenandoah, VA. Died, 28 Feb 1891, in Race Track, Powell, MT, age 72. She married John FIFER, 1839, in VA. Born, 1818, in VA. Resided in Scotland, MO in 1850.

29 ix. Milton Turner SMITH. Born, 1820, in Shenandoah, VA. Died in Shenandoah, VA.

30 x. Frances Marinda SMITH. Born, 1822, in Shenandoah, VA. Died in OH.

31 xi. Haidee Angeline SMITH. Born, 8 Feb 1826, in Shenandoah, VA. Died, 8 Dec 1915, in Vale, Malheur, OR, age 89. Buried at Deer Lodge, Powell, MT. She married, first, James ROSEBOROUGH, 1 Mar 1855, in Scotland, MO. She married, second, John JONES. Killed by lightning in MT.

7. **John Meredith² TURNER** (John Meridy, 1). Born, 1787, in Fauquier, VA. Died, 15 Feb 1853, in Arbela, Scotland, MO, age 65 years.

He married Harriet COOKE, daughter of Charles COOKE and Mary LEGG, 3 Apr 1817, in Fauquier, VA by Rev. Thornton STRINGFELLOW, Baptist.[31] Born, 8 Jul 1799, in Fauquier, VA. Died, 8 Jan 1876, in Arbela, Scotland, MO, age 79 years 6 months. Both were buried in the Hickory Grove Cemetery.

The marriage bond, dated 29 March 1817, for John TURNER and Harriet COOKE was signed with John's mark and Charles COOKE'S signature. Since Harriet was not yet 18, Charles COOKE signed a consent for his daughter on the same day.[32] John TURNER was living with his mother in Fauquier on the 1810 and 1820 census. On the 1830 census he was listed with 2 sons and 4 daughters and no slaves.[33] The family was on the 1840 and 1850 census in Licking Co., Ohio and Harriet was on the 1860 census in Scotland Co., Missouri living with her daughter and son-in-law, Martha and Levi PRYOR.[34] In 1870 she was living with Samuel MARTIN and his family in Knox Co., Missouri after the recent death of her daughter, Kitty Ann MARTIN.[35]

On the 21 November 1850, John TURNER, age 66 years, a resident of Licking County, Ohio swore that he was "a private soldier in the company commanded by William DULING in the 84th regiment of militia commanded by Enoch RENO in the war with great Britain declared by the United States on the 18th day of June 1812, Drafted at Jermantown, Faquier County, Virginia on or about the 15th day of June A.D. 1812 for the term of six months and continued in actual service in said war for the term of six months and was honorably discharged at Ellicoats Mills [Maryland] on or about the 15th day of December A.D. 1812." His purpose was to obtain bounty land granted by an act passed 28 September 1850. He signed by mark. He was awarded 40 acres.

On the 28 March 1855, Harriett TURNER, age 58 years, a resident of the County of Scotland in the State of Missouri, declared that "she is the widow of John M. TURNER deceased." Her declaration contained the same information, except she said that he had volunteered at German Town in Fauquier County 26 August 1814 and served until the end of November 1814. The statement from the Treasury Department dated 9 June 1851 had confirmed that John TURNER'S service was from 25 Aug. 1814 to 24 Nov. 1814.

"She further states that she was married to the said John M. TURNER in Fauquier County in the State of Virginia on the 3rd day of April AD 1817 by the Rev. Thorton STRINGFELLOW, a minister of the Gospel and that her name before her said marriage was Harriett COOK, that her said Husband died at the County of Scotland in the State of Missouri on the 11th day of February AD 1854, and that she is still a widow."

Her purpose was to obtain bounty land granted by an act passed 3 March 1855. She signed by signature "Harriet Turner." She was awarded 120 acres. Levi C. PRYOR and John M. T. SMITH, residents of Scotland County, made affidavit to her statement. The record in the Family Bible was used to prove the marriage and was sworn to by Charles D. TURNER.[36]

On the 21 February 1854 Harriet TURNER of Scotland County, Missouri deposed that her husband died without a will and that she would administer the estate. The heirs were Betsey CROSS, Mary MARTIN, Francis TROUT, Martha PRIOR, Kitty Ann MARTIN, John TURNER, Charles TURNER, Thomas TURNER and Harriet TURNER widow, all of whom resided in Scotland County and Harriet LIVINGSTON who resided in Licking Co., Ohio.

Included in the probate file was a handwritten agreement by John M. TURNER for a bond dated 26 December 1852 for a deed to David TROUT to a tract of land in Scotland County, the "west half of the southeast fourth of the northeast quarter of section 4, township 65, range 10 west." It was attested by Alexander SMITH.

James P. KNOTT, clerk at the sale of the property of John M. TURNER on 14 March 1854 submitted the following sales list:

"A Bill of the sale of the property belonging to the Estate of John M. TURNER deceased made by Harriet TURNER Administratrix of the said Estate on the 14th day of March AD 1854 showing the property sold, the purchasers names, the amount paid for each article and the whole amount of sales.

Property sold	Names of Purchasers	Amount
1 single tree	**John Turner**	.35
2 chains	**Same**	.45
1 chain & 2 irons	**Same**	.15
2 Breast chains	**Same**	.25
1 Clivis & ring	**Same**	.30
1 pair Wagon lines	**David Trout**	1.70

1 " Harness	John Turner	.15
1 Bridle	Silas Martin	.35
1 Manure Fork	Chs. Turner	1.15
1 Blind Bridle	Daniel Trout	1.30
1 pair Wagon harness	Jefferson Collins	2.25
2 Corn Knives	Same	.35
1 Madan	Samuel Martin	.80
1 Axe	Chs. Turner	.30
1 Wagon Whip	Jno. Turner	.25
1 iron Wedge	Daniel Trout	.70
5 Meal Bags	Samuel Martin	.75
2 Meal Bags	Chs. Turner	.30
1 Plow Do	John Turner	.50
1 pair harness	Daniel Trout	2.25
1 Blind Bridle	Jno. Turner	.95
1 Harrow	Jefferson Collins	6.05
3 hogs	Chs. Turner	9.05
1 sow & shoats	Ben Bron?	8.60
1 Barrel	Michael Tucker	.45
20 bushel corn	Peter Lorin?	5.00
20 Do Do	Silas Martin	4.00
20 Do Do	Silas Martin	4.40
20 Do Do	Chs. Turner	5.00
20 Bu Corn	Chas. Turner	4.40
1 Bee Stand	David Trout	3.40
1 Clock?	John Turner	5.05
1 Brown Mare	David Trout	101.00
1 Halter	Wm. McVey	.35
Whole Amount of Sales		$172.30

State of Missouri, County of Scotland: James P. KNOTT being duly sworn deposes and says he acted as clerk at the sale of the property of John M. TURNER decd made by Harriet TURNER admx of said Estate on the 14th day of March AD 1854..."[37]

Children of John Meredith and Harriet COOKE TURNER:

+ 32 i. Elizabeth "Betsy"[3] TURNER.
+ 33 ii. Mary TURNER.
+ 34 iii. Sarah Frances TURNER.
+ 35 iv. Harriet TURNER.
+ 36 v. Martha M. TURNER.
+ 37 vi. Hannah Louise "Kitty Ann" TURNER.
+ 38 vii. John D. TURNER.
+ 39 viii. Charles Daniel TURNER.
+ 40 ix. Thomas Lee TURNER.

AHNENTAFEL CHART FOR HARRIET COOKE

1 Harriet COOKE, b. 8 Jul 1799 in Fauquier, VA, d. 8 Jan 1876 in Arbela, Scotland, MO, m. 3 Apr 1817 in Fauquier, VA, **John Meredith TURNER**.

PARENTS

2 Charles COOKE, b. before 1775, m. 21 Jul 1798 in Fauquier, VA.

3 Mary LEGG, b. before 1782 in VA.

GRANDPARENTS

6 William LEGG, b. before 1759 in Prince William, VA, d. 22 Jul 1833 in Culpeper, VA.

GREAT GRANDPARENTS

12 [Unknown] LEGG, b. after 1722 in Richmond, VA, d. in VA.

2ND GREAT GRANDPARENTS

24 Thomas LEGG, b. before 1693, d. after 1750 in Prince William, VA, m. before 1713 in Richmond, VA.

25 Sarah DAVENPORT, b. circa 1693 in VA, d. before 1734 in Richmond, VA.

3RD GREAT GRANDPARENTS

50 George DAVENPORT, b. before 1673, d. Mar 1735 in Richmond, VA, m. 1693 in Lancaster, VA.

51 Ruth SYDNOR, b. 24 Aug 1676 in Lancaster, VA, d. before 1735 in Richmond, VA.

4TH GREAT GRANDPARENTS

100 John DAVENPORT, b. in England?, d. Mar 1684 in Lancaster, VA, m. before 1672 in VA.

101 Margaret [UNKNOWN], b. before 1653 in England, d. after 1680 in Eng. or VA.

102 Fortunatus SYDNOR, b. in Eng. or VA, d. 1683 in Lancaster, VA.

103 Joanna [UNKNOWN], b. in England, d. in England.

NOTES: CHAPTER 2 - SECOND GENERATION

---

1 *Atlas of Muskingum County, Ohio* (New York: Beers, Soule & Co., 1866), p. 3.

2 Licking County, Ohio Deeds, GG:476.

3 Licking County, Ohio Deeds, 60:424-425.

4 Evelyn Cook Hall, *The Cook Book, John Wesley Cook and his Descendants* (Nevada, IA: 1975).

5 Fauquier County, Virginia, Personal Property Tax Books 1797-1807, 1820-1832; Land Tax Lists 1816-1834; Culpeper County, Virginia, Personal Property Tax Lists 1824-1838; microfilm at the Virginia State Library, Richmond, VA.

6 Martin, *Martin Family History*, p. 18.

7 Gott, *Fauquier Marriage Bonds*, p. 25.

8 *Ibid.*, p. 150.

9 *Ibid.*, p. 24.

10 John K. Gott, *Fauquier County, Virginia Guardian Bonds 1759-1871* (Bowie, MD: Heritage Books, 1990), p. 25; Gott, *Fauquier Marriage Bonds*, p. 130; Martin, *Martin Family History*, p. 29.

11 Gott, *Fauquier Guardian Bonds*, p. 37.

12 Gott, *Fauquier Marriage Bonds*, p. 151.

13 1810 Fauquier County, Virginia Census, p. 272; 1820 Fauquier County, Virginia Census, p. 79; 1830 Fauquier County, Virginia Census, p. 417.

14 1840 Licking County, Ohio Census, p. 219.

15 Martin, *Martin Family History*, p. 18.

16 Gott, *Fauquier Marriage Bonds*, p. 203.

17 *Fauquier County Historical Society Bulletin*, 1:337.

18 Emalie Fletcher Ewing, *My Turner Family*, (unpublished 1969)

19 John Vogt & T. William Kethley, Jr., *Virginia Historic Marriage Register: Shenandoah County Marriage Bonds, 1772-1850* (Athens, GA: Iberian Press, 1984), p. 401.

20 *Ibid.*

21 Gott, *Fauquier Marriage Bonds*, p. 186; Gott, *Fauquier Guardian Bonds*, p. 8.

22 John K. Gott, *Abstracts of Fauquier County, Virginia Wills, Inventories and Accounts 1759 - 1800*, (John Gott, 1976), pp. 1, 14, 27.

23 Gott, *Fauquier Guardian Bonds*, pp. 2, 3, 8.

24 Fauquier County Deeds, 15:512.

25 Ewing, *My Turner Family*, pp. 9-23.

26 "The founder of the LEHEW family in Virginia was Nicholas LEHEW, a Huguenot who escaped after the Revocation of the Edict of Nantes to England concealed in a hogshead. He settled

in Northumberland County on a tobacco plantation prior to 1710. His sole heir Peter LEHEW and his wife Frances moved with their children in 1724 to Stafford County near Manassas, where he bought 927 acres adjoining Mann PAGE'S land. Some twenty years later the family crossed the mountain and settled on Great Happy Creek on land now embraced in Front Royal. One or more of their sons fought in the French and Indian War. For a number of years the town was called LeHewtown, after Peter's son Spencer who established the first Sunday School in this neighborhood." Carrie Esther Spencer, et al. *A Civil War Marriage in Virginia* (Boyce, VA: Carr, 1956) p. 5.

27 Ewing, *My Turner Family*, p. 12.

28 Vogt & Kethley, *Shenandoah Marriage Bonds*, pp. 150, 200.

29 Gott, *Fauquier Marriage Bonds*, p. 157.

30 Vogt & Kethley, *Shenandoah Marriage Bonds*, p. 386.

31 Gott, *Fauquier Marriage Bonds*, p. 203.

32 Marriage Bonds of Fauquier County, 3:319.

33 1830 Fauquier County, Virginia Census, p. 460.

34 1840 Licking County, Ohio Census, p. 219; 1850 Licking County, Ohio Census, p. 719; 1860 Scotland County, Missouri Census, p. 169.

35 1870 Knox County, Missouri Census, p. 23.

36 National Archives, War of 1812 Bounty Land Record for John M. TURNER, WT 24380-120-55-1812.

37 Scotland County, Missouri, Probate Court, File 87, Case number 147.

CHAPTER 3

THE THIRD GENERATION

By 1851 most of the related TURNER and SMITH families had left Ohio and migrated further west to Missouri. Only Peter and Harriet LIVINGSTON(35) remained in Ohio. The OLIVERS(12) and part of the MARTIN(9)(87) family moved to Parke County, Indiana.

The TURNER and SMITH families were not the first settlers on the Missouri frontier, but they did arrive in time to receive government land. William H. TURNER(13) patented land in Scotland County in 1836, 1839 and 1840.[1] Michael MILLER(19) patented land in 1839 and 1840.[2] Daniel M. SMITH(26) patented land in 1838 and Lewis T. J. SMITH(27) and Alexander SMITH(25) patented land in 1839.[3]

John Meredith Turner SMITH(21) (who reported that he settled in Scotland County in 1842) surrendered a Land Warrant for 160 acres in 1850.[4]

Shortly after John Meredith TURNER(7) arrived in Missouri in 1851, he presented his War of 1812 Bounty Land Warrant to the nearest U.S. Land Agent in Palmyra on 10 November 1851 and received 40 acres in Harrison Twp., near Arbela.[5] On that same day, five others in the family transacted land deeds: Michael CROSS(32), Willis MARTIN(33), Levi PRYOR(36), Lewis SMITH(27) and Alexander TURNER(16). They received title to 400 acres of land, some selling for as little as 50 cents an acre.

After the death of John Meredith TURNER(7), in 1855 Harriet COOKE TURNER received a warrant for an additional 120 acres which she signed over to her son John M. TURNER(38).[6] He received 120 acres in Adair County on the border of Knox County, a distance south by 25 miles from the other families near Arbela and Etna.[7] Besides John D. TURNER(38) and his family, Charles Daniel TURNER(39) was living in Salt River Township in Adair County with his family and his youngest brother, Thomas Lee TURNER(40) on the 1860 census.[8]

In November of 1861, Confederate General Sterling PRICE issued a proclamation "To the People of Central and Northern Missouri" appealing for fifty thousand men. Many southern sympathizers responded to this call. The Confederates were unwilling to risk troops north of the Missouri River so all they did was to harass the Union troops in that section and push forward the enlistment of men for PRICE'S army. During the winter of 1862 many Federal troops left Northeast Missouri and the Confederates took advantage of their absence.

Col. John PORTER, who had been a farmer in Knox County before the war, recruited over 5,000 Confederate soldiers from Northeast Missouri in a little over a half year. After several brilliant victories, on 31 July 1862 at Kirksville he was soundly defeated by the badly outnumbered Union force of General MCNEIL. Recruiting for the South in that section after August 6 was hazardous due to the presence of Federal troops. On August 8 PORTER was driven into southeast Adair County where his men deserted so rapidly that barely five hundred remained with him. He retreated south.[9]

John D., Charles Daniel, and Thomas Lee TURNER were living in Adair County in 1860. Before 1862 Charles Daniel TURNER(39) also retreated south, or at least sent his family south, as his son Jefferson Davis TURNER(128) was born in Sedalia, Pettis County in January of 1862. The only Confederate service record found for Charles TURNER was an enlistment in Boone County, Missouri on 21 September 1862 as a Pvt. in Company A, SNIDER'S Battalion, Missouri Cavalry.[10]

The biography of James T. TURNER(46) says that "He was a soldier in the late war."[11] They did not say which side. There is no Union pension record for him, so he may have been a Confederate. Not all of the family sympathies were for the South. John T. CROSS(79) (son of Michael), served in the Union Army. He enlisted in Company A, 19th Iowa Volunteer Infantry.[12]

During the war, life was very difficult in Northeast Missouri. After the battles of 1862, hostilities in Northeast Missouri ended except for the guerrilla warfare waged by such men as Bill ANDERSON and Bill QUANTRILL. They were savage and merciless in their methods and were largely thieves and murderers attacking both sides. There is a story in John D. TURNER'S(38) family of seeing QUANTRILL'S Raiders. A son of William and Ann NORTHCRAFT(24) was taken from his home, shot, and left by the side of the road 8 November 1862.[13]

In the summer of 1865, the three sons of John Meredith TURNER [John D.(38), Charles Daniel(39) and Thomas Lee(40)] and the one son of Daniel Meridy TURNER [James Daniel(20)] left Missouri for Oregon. The biographer of John D. TURNER states, "In 1865 they crossed the plains with ox teams to Oregon, being six months in making the journey." His son, Joseph A. TURNER, was born in August of 1865 on the Oregon Trail. John D. TURNER and James Daniel TURNER went to Yamhill County. Charles TURNER and Thomas TURNER settled in Clackamas County. The remainder of the third generation of the family stayed in northeast Missouri.

MAP OF MISSOURI

SCOTLAND AND CLARK
ADAIR AND KNOX
COUNTIES

MAP OF PROPERTY IN MISSOURI

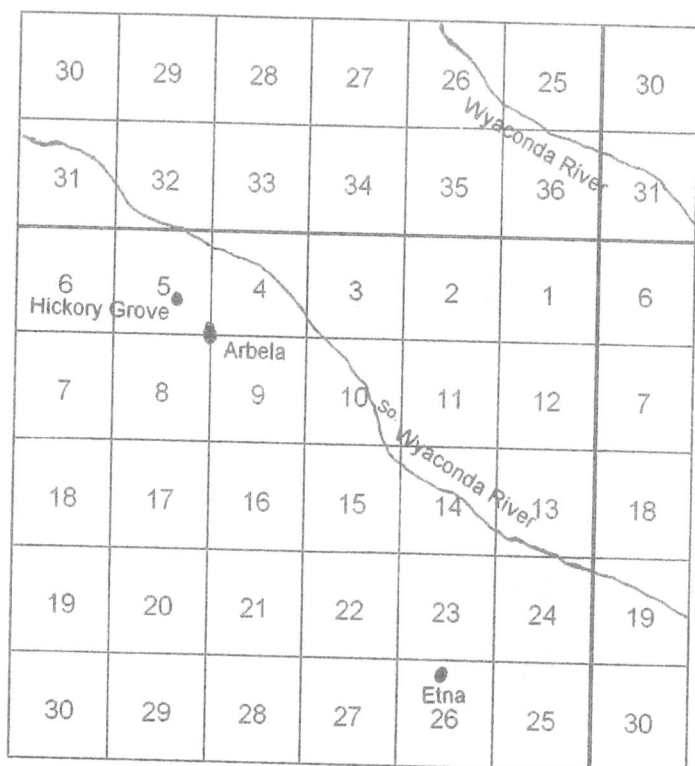

T.66N.R.10W. T.66N.R.9W.

30	29	28	27	26	25	30
31	32	33	34	35	36	31
6 Hickory	5 Grove	4	3	2	1	6
7	8	Arbela 9	10	11	12	7
18	17	16	15	14	13	18
19	20	21	22	23	24	19
30	29	28	27	Etna 26	25	30

Wyaconda River
So. Wyaconda River

T.65N.R.10W. T.65N.R.9W.

SCOTLAND COUNTY MISSOURI
Land that was owned by members of the TURNER family.

Sources:
Deed Books of Scotland County, Missouri.
Bounty Land Warrant #9919 issued 17 Jun 1851 by the U.S. Government in Washington D.C. for the service of John M. TURNER in the War of 1812. John TURNER filed his application with the Justice of the Peace, Thomas D. FLEMING, Perryton, Licking, OH on 30 Nov 1850 and the Warrant was surrendered at Palmyra, MO at the U. S. Land Office on 10 Nov 1851. He received 40 acres in Section 4, Township 65N, Range 10W in Harrison Township, Scotland County, Missouri.

LAND RECORDS OF MISSOURI

SECTION TOWNSHIP RANGE	ACRES	DATE	NAME
S 3 T65N R10W	80A	1838	Daniel M. SMITH
S 3 T65N R10W	80A	1850	John M. T. SMITH
S 3 T65N R10W	80A	1850	John M. T. SMITH
S 4 T65N R10W	80A	1839	Lewis T. J. SMITH
S 4 T65N R10W	40A	1839	Alexander SMITH
S 4 T65N R10W	40A	1839	Alexander SMITH
S 4 T65N R10W	48A	1839	Alexander SMITH
S 4 T65N R10W	40A	1851	John M. TURNER
S 4 T65N R10W	40A	1853	John M. TURNER
S 5 T65N R10W	85A		Wm F. NORTHCRAFT
S 5 T65N R10W	40A	1839	Alexander SMITH
S 6 T65N R10W	142A	1838	James TURNER
S 6 T65N R10W	43A	1838	James TURNER
S 8 T65N R10W	80A		Benjamin POWER
S 8 T65N R10W	40A	1853	John TURNER
S 9 T65N R10W	80A	1853	John TURNER
S 9 T65N R10W	40A	1853	John TURNER
S 9 T65N R10W	40A	1853	Samuel MARTIN
S 9 T65N R10W	40A	1854	John TURNER
S10 T65N R10W	40A	1840	Wm. H. TURNER
S10 T65N R10W	80A	1851	Levi C. PRYOR
S10 T65N R10W	40A	1854	Levi C. PRYOR
S11 T65N R10W	40A	1853	Wm. A. TURNER
S14 T65N R10W	160A		Hosea ANDERSON
S14 T65N R10W	80A	1856	Silas MARTIN
S15 T65N R10W	80A		Hosea ANDERSON
S15 T65N R10W	120A	1836	William TURNER
S15 T65N R10W	120A	1840	Michael MILLER
S16 T65N R10W	120A		Benjamin POWER
S16 T65N R10W	40A		W. A. TURNER
S16 T65N R10W	40A		John. M. T. SMITH
S22 T65N R10W	120A	1839	William TURNER
S22 T65N R10W	40A	1851	Lewis T. SMITH
S23 T65N R10W	80A		Hosea ANDERSON
S23 T65N R10W	80A	1851	Lewis T. SMITH
S23 T65N R10W	40A	1851	Willis MARTIN
S23 T65N R10W	40A	1851	Alexander TURNER
S23 T65N R10W	40A	1853	Michael CROSS
S23 T65N R10W	40A	1853	Wm. MARTIN
S23 T65N R10W	40A	1854	Wm. TURNER
S24 T65N R10W	160A	1839	Michael MILLER
S24 T65N R10W	80A	1851	Michael CROSS

THIRD GENERATION

13. **William H.³ TURNER** (Daniel Meridy, 4). Born, 8 Nov 1799, in Fauquier, VA. Died, 26 Dec 1879, in Scotland, MO, age 80.

He married, first, Mary MCKAY, 3 Sep 1824, in Shenandoah, VA.[14] Born, 12 Apr 1787, in VA. Died, 23 Nov 1854, in Scotland, MO, age 67. Between 1832 and 1835 they moved from Shenandoah, VA to OH. William TURNER had land patents in 1836 and 1839 in Scotland, MO. They were both buried in the Power Cemetery, near Arbela. Children:

+	41	i.	William A.⁴ TURNER.
	42	ii.	Charles W. TURNER. Born, 21 Sep 1830, in Shenandoah, VA. Died, 3 Nov 1864, in Scotland, MO, age 34. Buried in the Power Cemetery.
	43	iii.	John L. TURNER. Born, 2 Jan 1832, in Shenandoah, VA. Died, 9 Mar 1854, in Scotland, MO, age 22. Buried in the Power Cemetery.
	44	iv.	Henry H. TURNER. Born, 1835, in OH.

He married, second, Harriet [UNKNOWN] TOWNSEND, 27 May 1856, in Clark, MO. She was not listed with William on the 1860 census. He was living with his son, William A. TURNER in Jefferson, Scotland, MO.

15. **Ann H. (Nancy)³ TURNER** (Daniel Meridy, 4). Born, 1806, in Fauquier, VA.

She married, first, Thomas H. JESSE, 8 Sep 1842, in Scotland, MO. Died, before 1850, in Scotland, MO. Nancy JESSE was living with William H. TURNER on the 1850 census in Harrison, Scotland, MO. Child:

45 i. Lewis⁴ JESSE. Born, 1847, in Scotland, MO.

She married, second, Amos DENHAM, 16 Apr 1854, in Clark, MO.

16. **Alexander S.[3] TURNER** (Daniel Meridy, 4). Born, 1809, in Shenandoah, VA. Died, Aug 1856, in Scotland, MO, age 47. Buried in the Etna Cemetery.

He married Elizabeth ANDERSON, daughter of Hosea ANDERSON and Clarinda ALLINGTON, 19 Dec 1839, in Clark, MO. Born, Jan 1820, in OH or KY. Died, after 1900, in Clark, MO. She is on the 1900 Clark, MO census living with her son John A. TURNER where she is listed as age 80, born Kentucky.

"Elizabeth ANDERSON was born in Sangamon County, Illinois, near Springfield, a daughter of Hosea ANDERSON, of English descent and a pioneer settler of Illinois. At one time Mrs. TURNER'S mother was captured by the Indians but her life was saved by the chief, who admired her for her long hair and beautiful face and form. Alexander TURNER and wife were among the early settlers of Scotland County, Missouri. He had been a farmer all his life, and held important offices in the county."[15] Children:

+ 46 i. James T.[4] TURNER.
+ 47 ii. Mary Frances TURNER.
+ 48 iii. Martha Ann TURNER.
+ 49 iv. John Alexander TURNER.
+ 50 v. Nancy L. TURNER.
51 vi. William Richard TURNER. Born, 1856, in Scotland, MO. Died, 1875, in Scotland, MO, age 19.

18. **Lewis[3] TURNER** (Daniel Meridy, 4). Born, 1815, in Shenandoah, VA. Died, before 1870 when his widow was living alone, in Scotland, MO.

He married Rebecca WOOD, 15 Mar 1840, in Clark, MO. Born, 1823, in KY. Died, 1874 according to the Bear Creek Baptist Church records, in Scotland, MO, age 51. Children:

52 i. George[4] TURNER. Born, 1842, in MO.
+ 53 ii. Mary M. TURNER.
54 iii. Symanthy TURNER. Born, 1847, in MO. She married John Franklin JOHNSON, 28 Apr 1865, in Clark, MO.
55 iv. Martha C. TURNER. Born, 1849, in MO. She married Socrates BIRCHUM, 25 Apr 1869, in Clark, MO.
56 v. Demarious TURNER. Born, 26 Sep 1851, in MO. Died, 9 Jul 1936, in Clark, MO, age 86. She is on

the 1900 Wyaconda, Clark, MO census as a dressmaker. Buried at Wyaconda Cemetery.

+ 57 vi. Andrew Jackson TURNER.

58 vii. James B. TURNER. Born, 1857, in MO.

59 viii. C. P. "Brookenridge" TURNER. Born, 1860, in MO.

19. **Maria Louisa[3]** TURNER (Daniel Meridy, 4). Born, 19 Mar 1819, in Shenandoah, VA. Died, 13 Jul 1897, in Scotland, MO, age 78. Buried in the Memphis Cemetery.

She married, first, Michael MILLER, 10 Apr 1838, in Coshocton, OH. Born, 1812, in OH. Died, 1852, in Scotland, MO, age 40. Children:

60 i. Elizabeth[4] MILLER. Born, 1840, in MO. She married [Unknown] DOBYNS.

61 ii. Mary Angeline MILLER. Born, 1842, in MO.

62 iii. Charles S. MILLER. Born, 1844, in MO. Died, 1890, age 46.

63 iv. William MILLER. Born, 1846, in MO.

64 v. Nancy MILLER. Born, Nov 1849, in MO.

65 vi. Martin MILLER. Born, 17 Aug 1851, in MO. Died, 1916, age 65. He married Matilda HAYDEN, 16 Dec 1875.

She married, second, Austin HUGHES, after 1852, in Scotland, MO. Born, 1811, KY. Child:

66 vii. John HUGHES. Born, 1861, in MO.

20. **James Daniel[3]** TURNER (Daniel Meridy, 4). Born, 12 Aug 1820, in Shenandoah, VA. Died, 27 Jun 1909, in Columbia, WA, age 88.

He married, first, Amanda M. ENSIGN, 25 Mar 1847, in Clark, MO. Born, 1822, in KY. Died, before 1856, in Clark, MO. She is probably the daughter of Justus and Elizabeth ENSIGNE who are on the 1850 Clark, MO census in the same district as James and Amanda TURNER. Children:

+ 67 i. Mary Elizabeth[4] TURNER.

68 ii. William J. "Bud" TURNER. Born, Dec 1848, in Clark, MO. Died, 23 Dec 1914, in Umatilla, OR,

age 66.

\+ 69 iii. Jane A. TURNER.

He married, second, Mary PINKERTON, daughter of David PINKERTON and Mary TURTLE, 7 Aug 1856, in Clark, MO. Born, 16 Apr 1838, in Barbersville, Knox, KY. Died, 2 Jun 1918, in Columbia, WA, age 80. Both buried in the Dayton Cemetery.

James TURNER is on the 1850 and 1860 census in Jefferson, Clark, MO and on the 1870 census in Monmouth, Polk, OR. "James TURNER died at home on upper 5th Street, Sunday morning, age 88 years, 10 months, 15 days. He was a native of West Virginia and came here in 1871."[16]

One obituary says "James D. TURNER, pioneer farmer of 1865 and one of the oldest men in Columbia County, died here Sunday, aged 89 years. Mr. TURNER had been failing in health for eight years and the end was expected. His death was due to senile decay. The funeral will be held at the home tomorrow at 2 o'clock, the Rev. W. H. HARRIS officiating. Burial will be in the Dayton Cemetery.

Mr. TURNER was a native of Virginia. He moved to Missouri and married Miss Mary PINKERTON. In 1865 the family crossed the plains to the Willamette Valley, Ore. Five years later [1871] they moved to Columbia County and Mr. TURNER took up a homestead near Alto. He moved to Dayton ten years ago.

Besides a wife, he is survived by seven children. They are Mrs. Mary E. PRICE, Adams, Ore.; W. J. TURNER, Pilot Rock, Ore.; Mrs. Jane WALLAN, Adams, Ore.; Mrs. Eliza ANDERSON, Wenatchee; Mrs. Amanda REDFORD, Dayton; Sidney LUKENBEAL, Waitsburg; Mrs. Anna LINDLEY, Dayton."[17] Children:

\+ 70 iv. Sarah Elizabeth TURNER.

71 v. Amanda F. TURNER. Born, 23 Jul 1859, in Scotland, MO. Died, 13 Aug 1942, in Columbia, WA, age 83. She married John B. REDFORD, 20 Dec 1874, in Walla Walla, WA, by John H. WATSON, M.G. The witnesses were James TURNER and Joseph BALDWIN. Born, 31 Dec, 1846. Died, 3 Apr 1909, Columbia, WA, age 62. Both were buried in the Dayton Cemetery. "After a short illness of but a few weeks, J. B. REDFORD, one of Dayton's oldest residents died at his home on Fourth Street Saturday evening at 7 o'clock, age 62 years, 3

months, 2 days. Mr. REDFORD was a native of Missouri and came west in 1865 and was a school teacher for many years after which he took up the vocation of farming. The deceased is survived by his wife, two sisters -- Mrs. L. ISRAEL of California and Mrs. Martha AYRES of this County and one brother E. REDFORD of Cottage Grove, Oregon. Funeral was held from the Christian Church."[18] It was reported in 1882 that John B. REDFORD owned 360 acres 6 miles south of Dayton where he was a farmer. He was born in Warsaw, Benton, MO, 31 Dec 1846 and came to Grand Ronde, OR in 1864 and to Columbia County in 1872.[19]

72 vi. Anga Samantha TURNER. Born, 23 Jul 1859, in Scotland, MO. Died, 20 Feb 1860, in Scotland, MO, age 6 months.

73 vii. Nancy Price TURNER. Born, 22 Nov 1861, in Scotland, MO. Died, 28 Oct 1874, in Columbia, WA, age 12. Buried in the Bundy Cemetery.

\+ 74 viii. Sidney Bell TURNER.

75 ix. James H. Born, 17 Jun 1868, in Yamhill, OR. Died, 18 Jan 1879, in Columbia, WA, age 10. Buried in the Bundy Cemetery.

\+ 76 x. Mary "Emma" TURNER.

\+ 77 xi. Anna Bertha TURNER.

32. **Elizabeth "Betsy"[3] TURNER** (John Meredith, 7). Born, 9 Jun 1818, in Fauquier, VA.

She married Michael CROSS, circa 1838, in Licking, OH. Born, 1818, in Muskingum, OH. They were on the 1850 census in Hopewell, Muskingum, OH and the 1860 census in Harrison, Scotland, MO. Michael CROSS bought land from the government in 1851 and 1853 near Etna, Scotland, MO.[20]

"Michael CROSS, carpenter, Agency City, Iowa. Born 1818 in Muskingum County, Ohio. In 1850 he came to Missouri and in 1861 to Wapello County, Iowa. He owns 114 acres of land in Agency Township, also property in the city. He was Justice of the Peace from 1872 to 1874 and is now elected to serve from 1878 to 1880. Our subject was president of the school board serving from 1874 to 1877. Mr. CROSS has been Township Treasurer for six terms. He married Elizabeth TURNER in 1839. She was born 9 June 1818 in Fauquier County, Virginia. They have nine children, four living:

John T., practicing physician in Farmington, Van Buren County and graduating in 1865 from Keokuk Medical College; Etna V., now Mrs. AMOS; Michael W. and Jessie H. John T. enlisted in 1862, Co. A, 19th I.V.I. served to the end of the war, part of the time on hospital duty at Keokuk. He is a Republican and they are members of the Baptist Church."[21] Children:

78 i. William H.[4] CROSS. Born, 1839, in Licking, OH. Died, 1840, in Licking, OH, age 1. Buried in the Gratiot Cemetery in Hopewell township.

79 ii. John Thomas CROSS. Born, 30 May 1841, in Licking, OH. Died, 28 Jan 1913, in Van Buren, IA, age 71. Buried in the Farmington Cemetery. He married Lydia BEHME, daughter of Anton BEHME, before 1870. Born, 21 Jan 1844, in Lee, IA. Died, 7 May 1931, in Farmington, Van Buren, IA, age 87.

80 iii. Harriet CROSS. Born, 1844, in Licking, OH.

81 iv. Mary F. CROSS. Born, 1846, in Licking, OH.

82 v. Martha Louise CROSS. Born, 1848, in Licking, OH. Died, 29 Sep 1865, age 17, in Wapello, IA. Buried at the Agency Cemetery.

83 vi. Ruth H. CROSS. Born, Jul 1850, in Licking, OH. Died, before 1860, in Scotland, MO.

84 vii. Etna Virginia CROSS. Born, 1855, in Scotland, MO. She married Philip AMOS, 17 Aug 1873, in Wapello, IA. Born 1847 in PA.

85 viii. Michael Webster CROSS. Born, 1857, in Scotland, MO.

86 ix. Jesse H. CROSS. Born, 1860, in Scotland, MO. He married Rose L. [UNKNOWN], before 1887. Born, 1867, in IL.

33. Mary[3] TURNER (John Meredith, 7). Born, 22 May 1821, in Fauquier, VA. Died, 3 Nov 1891, in Scotland, MO, age 70.[22]

She married William Willis MARTIN, son of William MARTIN and Elizabeth W. BROWN(9), 1 Apr 1841, in Licking, OH.[23] Born, 1821, in VA. Died, 1896, in Scotland, MO, age 75.[24] Both were buried at the Hickory Grove Cemetery, Arbela.

Willis MARTIN migrated to Scotland, MO from Muskingum, OH about 1851. On the 1850 census he was living in Hopewell, Muskingum, OH. In 1851 he bought 40 acres of land in Scotland County from the U.S. Government. Later, in 1853, he bought an adjoining 20 acres from his brother-in-law, Michael CROSS.[25] This land was near the town of Etna, MO. Children:[26]

87 i. John W.[4] MARTIN. Born, 1842, in Licking, OH. Died, Dec 1895, in Parke, IN, age 53. He married Sarah Jane OLIVER, daughter of Samuel L. OLIVER(12) and Frances [UNKNOWN], 21 Jun 1863, in Parke, IN. Born, 1846, in Licking, OH.

88 ii. Martha Ann MARTIN. Born, Feb 1844, in Licking, OH. Died, circa 1928, in Clark, MO. She married James K. Polk DOCHTERMAN, circa 1860, in MO. Born, Jan 1845, in IA. Died, 1924, age 79. Both were buried at Luray, Clark, MO.

89 iii. Charles Thomas MARTIN. Born, 12 Jul 1852, in Scotland, MO. Died, 16 Mar 1895, in Scotland, MO, age 42. He married Emeline Neal THOMAS, 23 Dec 1875, in Scotland, MO. Born, 1 Jun 1858. Died, 20 Feb 1941, Scotland, MO, age 82. Buried at Hickory Grove Cemetery.

90 iv. Andy Jackson MARTIN. Born, circa 1854, in Scotland, MO. He married Lucy Ann SHOUDER, circa 1878, in MO. Born, 28 Nov 1859. Died, 21 Apr 1893, Scotland, MO, age 33. She was buried in Clay Bank Cemetery.

91 v. S. J. MARTIN. Born, 1856, in Scotland, MO.

34. **Sarah Frances[3] TURNER** (John Meredith, 7). Born, 22 Dec 1822, in Fauquier, VA. Died, 19 Mar 1889, in Scotland, MO, age 66. Buried at Hickory Grove Cemetery, near Arbela.

She married David TROUT, circa 1847, in Licking, OH. Born, 1818, in OH. Died, after 1880. There is a Nicholas TROUT age 75 born in VA living with them on the 1850 Bennington, Licking, OH census. They were on the 1860, 1870 and 1880 census in Harrison, Scotland, MO. Children:

92 i. Angeline[4] TROUT. Born, 1848, in Licking, OH. She married James R. MCCLINTOCK, 21 May 1882, in Scotland, MO.

93 ii. Emanuel TROUT. Born, 1849, in Licking, OH.

94 iii. Rebecca H. TROUT. Born, 1851, in Scotland, MO. She married W. L. CAMPBELL in MO. Born, 1846, KY.

95 iv. Noah T. TROUT. Born, 1857, in Scotland, MO. Died, 1942, in MO, age 85. Buried at Hickory

Grove Cemetery, near Arbela.

35. **Harriet[3] TURNER** (John Meredith, 7). Born, 1826, in Fauquier, VA.

She married Peter LIVINGSTON, circa 1846, in Licking, OH. Born, 1822, in OH. They were on the 1850, 1860 and 1880 census in Perry Twp, Licking, OH. Children, all born in Licking, OH:

96 i. Tobias[4] LIVINGSTON. Born, 1847.
97 ii. Martha LIVINGSTON. Born, 1849.
98 iii. Elizabeth LIVINGSTON. Born, 1851.
99 iv. Catherine LIVINGSTON. Born, 1855.
100 v. Mary M. LIVINGSTON. Born, 1859.
101 vi. Amelia LIVINGSTON. Born, 1863.
102 vii. Seward LIVINGSTON. Born, 1865.

36. **Martha M.[3] TURNER** (John Meredith, 7). Born, 21 Jan 1827, in Fauquier, VA. Died, 11 Sep 1905, in Columbia, WA, age 78 years 7 months 20 days, at the home of C. W. PRYOR.[27] Buried at the Dayton Cemetery.

She married Levi C. PRYOR, son of Frederick PRYOR and Tobitha WILKINS, circa 1847, in OH. (He had married Catherine ALBERT, 14 Mar 1839, Muskingum, OH[28] and had two children: Tobitha "Visa" E. born 1840 and Cecelia born 1844, both in OH.) Born, 6 Nov 1815, in OH. Died, 6 Apr 1900, in Scotland, MO, age 84. Buried in Hickory Grove Cemetery near Arbela. They are on the 1850 census in Jackson, Muskingum OH. He bought land in Section 10 of Scotland, MO in 1851 and 1854.[29] They are on the 1860 and 1870 census in Harrison, Scotland, MO.

The grandfather of Levi PRYOR, Timothy PRYOR, was originally from PA, but came to OH and settled on the Muskingum River about 1798. His son Frederick PRYOR was born in PA and was 11 years of age when he came to OH. He and his wife had 13 children, one of whom was Levi C. PRYOR.[30]

Charles W. PRYOR was in the 1887 Walla Walla census as a single man living near the WEATHERFORDS. There was a news article in the *Columbia County News* announcing the birth of his son 2 April 1895. In the news of 23 March 1895 it was reported that, "Grandma PRYOR who has been on a prolonged visit with relatives in and around Waitsburg, is now with her sons, C. W. and W. A. PRYOR."[31] She was on the 1900 census with Wm. A. PRYOR.

"Charles PRYOR and his younger brother Will came from Missouri in 1889. Charles bought a farm 1½ miles from Covello but kept it only a short time before selling it and buying another on the road to Dayton where the family of four children grew up. They were Eldon, William, Dwelly and Nellie. Will worked for his brother until he bought a farm just east of Whetstone. They also acquired additional land as PRYOR Bros. The Will PRYORS had a son, Forrest."[32] Children:

103 i. Dudley F.[4] PRYOR. Born, 7 Jan 1852, in Scotland, MO. Died, 31 May 1917, Luray, Clark, MO, age 65. He married Mary L. EVANS, 22 Jan 1874, in Scotland, MO. Born 1850, in KY.

104 ii. W. L. PRYOR. Born in Scotland, MO.[33]

105 iii. Amos F. PRYOR. Born, 16 Aug 1854, in Scotland, MO. Died, 28 Jun 1917, age 62 yrs, 10 m, 12 d, in Scotland, MO. He married Bertha J. TEETER, 24 Oct 1878, in Scotland, MO. Born, 1 Dec 1859, in MO. Died 2 Aug 1945.

106 iv. Charles Walter PRYOR. Born, Aug 1857, in Scotland, MO. Died, 12 Jul 1927, in Dayton, Columbia, WA, age 69. He married Sadie H. CAMP, before 1894. Born, Mar 1870, KS. Died, 7 Nov 1939, Dayton, Columbia, WA, age 69. Both were buried in the Dayton Cemetery.[34]

107 v. Emma PRYOR. Born, 1863, in Scotland, MO.

108 vi. William A. PRYOR. Born, 16 Mar 1866, in Scotland, MO. Died, 16 Mar 1916, in Dayton, Columbia, WA, age 50. He married Katie L. ALBRIGHT, 14 Mar 1888. Born, Feb 1867, IA.

37. **Hannah Louise "Kitty Ann"[3] TURNER** (John Meredith, 7). Born, 6 Aug 1830, in Fauquier, VA. Died, 16 Mar 1870, in Knox, MO, age 39.

She married Samuel Grandville MARTIN, son of William MARTIN and Elizabeth W. BROWN(9), circa 1849, in Licking, OH. Born, 9 Sep 1825, in VA. Died, 3 Feb 1879, in Knox, MO, age 53. Both were buried at Mt. Tabor Cemetery, near Hurdland.

Samuel G. MARTIN migrated in 1851 to Scotland, MO from Licking, OH with his brother William Willis MARTIN and other members of the TURNER family. Samuel MARTIN purchased 40 acres from John and Mary TURNER in 1853.[35] He lived there until 1864 when he moved to Knox County where he farmed until his death in 1879.[36]

"The MARTINS came from Missouri [to Washington State] in 1889 and settled at Whetstone. The parents originated in Virginia where they were neighbors of the TURNERS. Mason MARTIN'S mother was a sister of Ben TURNER'S father. A son of Mace, Dewey and his wife Alferetta live in Dayton where their son Dorsey operates the Dorsey Inn and Cafe. Charley MARTIN was the principal farmer in the MARTIN family. He sold his farm of 520 acres to Bill CARLTON about 1905 and retired. Dave MARTIN, father of Ruth BACON ran a livery stable in Dayton."[37] Children:

109 i. Joseph Warren[5] MARTIN. Born, 24 Nov 1850, in Muskingum, OH. Died, 11 Dec 1929, in Knox, MO, age 79. He married, first, Louisa Jane ROSS, 24 Dec 1871, in Knox, MO. Born, 12 Jun 1853. Died, 16 Jul 1893, age 50. Both were buried at Mt. Tabor Cemetery. He married, second, Amanda E. [UNKNOWN], after 1893, in Knox, MO. Born, 1867.

110 ii. Melissa Ann MARTIN. Born, 10 Jan 1852, in Scotland, MO. Died, 31 Oct 1932, in Dufur, Wasco, OR, age 80. She married John Steele MORRIS, 11 Sep 1873, in Knox, MO. Born, 14 Aug 1840, Wayne, KY. Died, 17 Oct 1903, Dayton, Columbia, WA, age 60. Both were buried at the Dayton Cemetery.

111 iii. William M. MARTIN. Born, 11 Apr 1855, in Scotland, MO. Died, 21 Feb 1936, in Knox, MO, age 80. He married, first, Sarah MUSGROVE OLIVER, daughter of William MUSGROVE and Mermelia MCLAUGHLIN, 26 Mar 1876, in Knox, MO. Born, 30 Jun 1836, Spencer, KY. Died, 3 Oct 1912, age 76. Both were buried at Mt. Tabor Cemetery. He married, second, Virginia TURNER SHEARER, daughter of Silas TURNER and Lou STACY and widow of Henry SHEARER, 14 Mar 1914, in Knox, MO. Born, 29 Jan 1859, Hannibal, MO. Died, 1931, age 72. He married, third, Amanda E. [UNKNOWN], widow of Joseph War-

ren MARTIN, 1932, in MO.

112 iv. Josiah Mason MARTIN.[38] Born, 28 Mar 1857, in Scotland, MO. Died, 5 May 1919, in Dayton, Columbia, WA, age 61. He came to Dayton in 1880. He married Celia STEELE, 7 Nov 1896, in Dayton, Columbia, WA. Born, Oct 1876, Coshocton, OH. Died, 19 Apr 1951, age 74. Both were buried at the Dayton Cemetery.

113 v. Henry T. MARTIN. Born, 27 May 1860, in Scotland, MO. Died, 22 May 1880, in Knox, MO, age 20. Buried, Mt. Tabor Cemetery.

114 vi. Charles Alexander MARTIN. Born, 21 Oct 1862, in Scotland, MO. Died, 3 Jul 1934, in Dayton, Columbia, WA, age 71. He married Christine Isabelle TETER, 21 Oct 1883, in Scotland, MO. Born, 21 Dec 1864, Scotland, MO. Died 19 Nov 1952, Dayton, WA, age 87.

115 vii. John David MARTIN. Born, 11 Mar 1865, in Knox, MO. Died, 11 Dec 1931, in Dayton, Columbia, WA, age 66. He married Anna Olive MORRIS, daughter of Samuel MORRIS and Jane Catherine BROWN, 6 Jun 1901, in Covello, Columbia, WA. Born, 29 Dec 1874, Springfield, MO. Died, 11 Jun 1924, Dayton, WA, age 49. Both buried at Dayton Cemetery.

116 viii. Harriet E. MARTIN. Born, 11 Mar 1865, in Knox, MO. Died of diphtheria, 11 Jun 1872, in Knox, MO, age 7. Buried at the Mt. Tabor Cemetery.

117 ix. Mary Frances MARTIN. Born, 14 Jul 1868, in Knox, MO. Died of pneumonia, 14 Feb 1898, in Dayton, Columbia, WA, age 29. She married William B. ABEL, 1889, in Dayton, Columbia, WA. Died, 19 Aug 1931, Dayton, Columbia, WA.

He married, second, (Mrs.) Margaret PATTEN, circa 1871, in Knox, MO. Born, 3 Jul 1833, in OH. Died, 9 Dec 1909, in Knox, MO, age 76. Buried at Mt. Tabor Cemetery. They had three children: Delphia Ann MARTIN, born 13 Mar 1872; Sherman MARTIN, born 15 Jun 1874; Elmer S. MARTIN, born 29 Dec 1878, all Knox, MO.

Samuel MARTIN made out a will 20 Jan 1879 and died two weeks later. The will in the courthouse is a copy, not the original.[39]

"I **Samuel G. Martin** Being of sound mind do make this my last (copy) will and Testament. first my funeral expenses paid, second to sel all of my personal property to pay my debts and the remainder to go to my Wife **Margaret** and my children and by her the number is three and I further bequeth to my wife **Margaret** as long as she remaines my Wider and my four youngest children here I name them **Mary Francis Martin**, **Delphy An Martin**, **Shearman Martin**, the infant not named and if my wife **Margaret** should marry, the Real estat to remain to my four children here above named, to use them until they arise to the age of fifteen my Real Estate. **Malissa An Moris**, **Josiah Mason Martin**, **Henry Martin**, **John Davis Martin**, **Mary Francis Martin**, **Delphy An Martin**, **Shearman Martin**, the infant not named. The eight children here above named to have Forty Dolars and one hundred lb of corn more tha the remainder of my children and I further bequeath to my wife **Margaret** when the youngest child arrives at the age of fifteen only to have forty acres it being SE NE Section 10 township one Range thirteen to have her life time or as long as she remains my wider and at the expiration of her time to be equally divided between my children. The remainder of My Real estate at the expiration of the fifteen years to be divided equally between my children. I **Samuel G. Martin** do make and apoint **James K. Henry** my exutor to carry out my last wil and testament this January 20 twentieth in the year of our lord Eighteen hundred and seventy nine.

Witness his
Hugh F. Henry **Samuel X Martin** (Seal)
John Pinkston mark"

AHNENTAFEL CHART FOR SAMUEL GRANDVILLE MARTIN

1 Samuel Grandville MARTIN, b. 9 Sep 1825 in VA, d. 3 Feb 1879 in Knox, MO, ma. circa 1849 in Licking, OH, Kitty Ann TURNER.

PARENTS
2 William MARTIN, b. 1792 in VA, d. 1863 in Parke, IN, ma. 26 Sep 1814 in Fauquier, VA.
3 Elizabeth W. BROWN(9), b. 1796 in Fauquier, VA, d. 1870 in Parke, IN.

GRANDPARENTS
6 Willis BROWN, d. before 1806 in Fauquier, VA, ma. 1 Oct 1791 in Fauquier, VA.
7 Elizabeth TURNER(3), b. 1771 in Fauquier, VA, d. 5 Oct 1839 in Licking, OH.

GREAT GRANDPARENTS
14 John Meridy TURNER(1), b. before 1747 in Prince William, VA, d. Jun 1815 in Fauquier, VA, ma. circa 1770 in Fauquier, VA.
15 Elizabeth [UNKNOWN], d. 1828 in Fauquier, VA.

---

38. **John D.**^{3} TURNER (John Meredith, 7). Born, 24 Feb 1831, in Fauquier, VA. Died, 20 Apr 1899, in Columbia, WA, age 68.[40] An article in the *Columbia County News* said, "Uncle John TURNER died at his residence Thursday morning, age 67. He came to this county in 1871 and settled on Whiskey Creek. He leaves property to his wife and four sons."[41]

He married Mary Ann POWER, daughter of Benjamin POWER and Hannah EVICK, 19 Jun 1853, in Scotland, MO. Born, 23 Feb 1829, in Vigo, IN. Died, 12 Feb 1911, in Columbia, WA, age 82. Both were buried in the Dayton Cemetery.

She married, first, Thomas ANDERSON (who was the brother of Elizabeth ANDERSON, who married Alexander S. TURNER(16) and had two children: William Franklin ANDERSON, born 11 Apr 1848 and Clarinda Jane ANDERSON, born 19 Feb 1850. William m. Sarah Eliza TURNER(70) and Clarinda m. Alexander PRICE, 23 Feb 1873. They are on the 1850, Washington, Clark, MO census. Alexander PRICE was the brother of John PRICE who m. Samantha TURNER(119).

After the marriage of Mary Ann POWER ANDERSON to John D. TURNER, they moved to Adair, MO where they are found in the 1860 census in Salt River township, Post Office, Wilson. In the 1870 census they are living in Dayton, Yamhill, OR.

"In 1865 they crossed the plains with ox teams to Oregon, being six months in making the journey. On their arrival they located in Yamhill county, that state, where they lived for about six years and in March, 1871, came to Washington. They took up their abode on Whiskey creek, in what is now Columbia county but was then a part of Walla Walla county, and the father preempted a quarter section of land, upon which he continued to reside until called to his final home."[42] Children:

+ 118 i. Benjamin M.^{4} TURNER.
+ 119 ii. Samantha Ann TURNER.
+ 120 iii. Harriet Antoinette TURNER.
+ 121 iv. John Thomas TURNER.
+ 122 v. James Patten TURNER.
+ 123 vi. Joseph A. TURNER.
+ 124 vii. Sydney Irene TURNER.
+ 125 viii. Charles M. TURNER.

CHARLES DANIEL TURNER
(1832-1917)

39. **Charles Daniel^3 TURNER** (John Meredith, 7). Born, 1 Jan 1832, in Licking, OH. Died, 26 Nov 1917, age 85, in Buckeye Township, Spokane, WA, at the home of his daughter Mary EVANS. The funeral home was in Rosalia, Whitman, WA. He was buried at Dayton, WA according to his death certificate, but no cemetery record was found.

He married, first, Sarah Elizabeth CROWN, daughter of William Sterling CROWN and Mary Magdalene BURRIER, 28 Dec 1854, in Clark, MO by Rev. John J. MARTIN. Born, 18 Feb 1835, in Muskingum, OH. Died, 6 Jul 1866, in Stafford, Clackamas, OR. She was buried in the Bird Cemetery. Her daughter, Harriet TURNER, said that her mother became sick on the Oregon Trail and prayed that she would make it to Oregon so that she would not be buried on the Trail. She was 31 years old when she died.

Sarah Elizabeth CROWN grew up in a large family of 12 children living in Muskingum, OH adjoining Licking, OH where Charles TURNER was raised. Her family moved to Van Buren, IA [adjoining Scotland and Clark, MO] in 1841 and her parents died there in 1878 and 1887. In the settlement of both of their estates, their daughter, Sarah E. TURNER, is named as deceased with children living in Washington Territory whose names were not known.[43]

In the 1860 census, Charles and Sarah TURNER were in Salt River Twp, Adair, MO with Charles' younger brother, Thomas Lee TURNER. When the Civil War began in 1861, Charles TURNER'S sympathies were with the Confederacy. He moved his family to Sedalia, Pettis, MO as the Union Army held most of northern Missouri. He named his son Jefferson Davis TURNER, born on 8 Jan 1862. There was one Confederate muster-in-roll for Charles TURNER in Boone County dated 21 Sep 1862.[44] He told his grandchildren many years later, that he hid in the well when the Bushwhackers recruited in his neighborhood. He never told about fighting in any battles. In the summer of 1865 Charles, with his brothers John and Thomas, and a cousin, James, and all of their wives and children left Missouri for Oregon. Children:

+ 126 i. Harriet Tabitha^4 TURNER.
  127 ii. Thomas D. TURNER. Born, 1859, in Knox, MO.
+ 128 iii. Jefferson Davis TURNER.
+ 129 iv. Mary Louisa TURNER.

He married, second, Marianna Eliza EVANS, daughter of William and Elizabeth EVANS, 3 Jan 1869, in Oregon City, Clackamas, OR.[45] Born, 28 Dec 1848, in MO. Died, 24 Jan 1889, in Columbia, WA, age 40. She was buried at the Bundy Hollow Cemetery. In 1870 they were living in Tualatin Precinct, Oregon City, Clackamas, OR. They moved to Columbia, WA, near Huntsville, about 1875, where Charles homesteaded. He later farmed near Turner. In the 1900 census he was living with his daughter, Lilly BIGGART, in Star Precinct., Columbia, WA. In 1910 he was living with his daughter, Mary EVANS, in Buckeye Township, Spokane, WA. Mary Louisa TURNER had married her step-mother's brother, John William EVANS, in 1881. The 1910 census has a question as to whether the person was a survivor of the Union or Confederate, Army or Navy. Charles D. TURNER, age 75, was listed as "CA" Confederate Army. Children:

	130	v.	Anna I. TURNER. Born, 7 Apr 1870, in Oregon City, Clackamas, OR. Died, 21 Jun 1873, in Clackamas, OR, age 3. Buried at Bird Cemetery, Stafford, next to the Charles' first wife.
+	131	vi.	Lilly Lenora TURNER.
+	132	vii.	Edward Daniel TURNER.
+	133	viii.	Vivian Winfred TURNER.
	134	ix.	Stella M. TURNER. Born, 16 Feb 1882, in Columbia, WA. Died, 5 Aug 1882, in Columbia, WA. Buried at the Bundy Cemetery.

AHNENTAFEL CHART FOR SARAH ELIZABETH CROWN

1 Sarah Elizabeth CROWN, b. 18 Feb 1835 in Muskingum OH, d. 6 Jul 1866 in Stafford, Clackamas, OR, m. 28 Dec 1854 in Clark, MO, **Charles Daniel TURNER**.

PARENTS

2 William Sterling CROWN, b. 8 Aug 1806 in Shenandoah, VA, d. 12 Apr 1878 in Farmington, Van Buren, IA, m. 1 Nov 1827 in Muskingum, OH.

3 Mary Magdalene BURRIER, b. 27 Aug 1806 in Frederick, MD, d. 31 Aug 1887 in Farmington, Van Buren, IA.

GRANDPARENTS

4 Joseph CROWN, b. circa 1777(?) in MD, d. before 1860 in Muskingum, OH, m. 26 Nov 1798 in Montgomery, MD.

5 Mary SLATER, b. 3 Mar 1776 in Piscataway, Prince George MD, d. 7 Aug 1852 in Muskingum, OH.

6 Adam BURRIER, b. circa 1765 in Frederick, MD, d. before 1830 in Frederick, MD, m. May 1793 in Frederick, MD.
7 Susanna SCHMIDT, b. 2 Oct 1774 in Frederick, MD, d. 1810 in Frederick, MD

GREAT GRANDPARENTS
8 Gerrard CROWN, b. circa 1756 in MD, d. Jul 1818 in Montgomery, MD, m. circa 1776 in MD. [Line not proven. Gerrard names a son, Joseph, in his will.]
9 Dorothy [UNKNOWN], b. in MD, d. in MD.
10 Richard SLATER, b. before 1750, d. before 1810 in Shenandoah, VA, m. circa 1772 in Prince George's, MD.
11 Jane [UNKNOWN]
12 Leonhard BURRIER, b. before 1740 in Germany, d. before 1800 in Woodsboro, Frederick, MD, m. before 1764 in Frederick, MD.
13 Barbara BOSTIAN, b. circa 1740 in New Hanover, Phila., PA, d. Apr 1815 in Woodsboro, Frederick, MD.
14 Johan Adam SCHMIDT, b. 4 Feb 1745/6 in Hochstenbac, Pfalz, Ger., d. 1823 in Frederick, MD, m. 25 May 1773 in Frederick, MD.
15 Regina NUSBAUM, b. circa 1753 in PA, d. after 1820 in Frederick, MD.

2ND GREAT GRANDPARENTS
16 Joseph CROWN, b. 1710, d. 1777 in Charles, MD, m. circa 1742 in Prince George's, MD.
17 Elizabeth DYER, b. 1726 in Prince George's, MD, d. 1776 in Prince George's, MD.
20 Richard SLATER, b. circa 1718, d. circa 1789 in Charles, MD.
26 Andreas BOSTIAN, b. Aug 1709 in Freinsheim, Pfalz, Ger., d. Jan 1789 in Frederick, MD, m. 27 Apr 1730 in New Hanover, Phila., PA.
27 Maria Albertina KRAUSS, b. circa 1708 in Germany, d. 28 Oct 1799 in Frederick, MD.
28 Johan Martin SCHMIDGEN, b. 1712 in Hochstenbac, Pfalz, Ger., d. Jan 1781 in Frederick, MD, m. 11 Sep 1739 in Hochstenbac, Pfalz, Ger.
29 Maria Catharina PEIFFER, b. 29 Mar 1712 in Hochstenbac, Pfalz, Ger., d. 8 Apr 1748 in Hochstenbac, Pfalz, Ger.
30 [Unknown] NUSBAUM, b. circa 1720 in Germany, d. before 1768 in PA or MD, m. before 1745 in PA.
31 Margaret [UNKNOWN], b. circa 1720 in Germany, d. after 1799 in Woodsboro, Frederick, MD.

3RD GREAT GRANDPARENTS

34 William DYER, b. 18 Nov 1705, d. 1754 in Prince George's, MD, m. 1725 in Prince George's, MD.

35 Susanna [UNKNOWN], b. 1701, d. after 1776 in Prince George's, MD.

52 Daniel SEBASTIAN, b. before 1679 in Germany, d. Aug 1725 in Freinsheim, Pfalz, Ger., m. before 1699 in Germany.

53 Eva Catharina [UNKNOWN], b. before 1679 in Germany, d. after 1716 in Freinsheim, Pfalz, Ger.

56 Adam SCHMIDGEN, b. 1681 in Hochstenbac, Pfalz, Ger., d. 20 May 1742 in Hochstenbac, Pfalz, Ger., m. 1703 in Hochstenbac, Pfalz, Ger.

57 [Unknown] VOHL, b. in Germany, d. 16 May 1757 in Hochstenbac, Pfalz, Ger.

58 Johann Thomas PEIFFER, b. in Germany, d. 1751 in Hochstenbac, Pfalz, Ger., m. 26 Jun 1711 in Hochstenbac, Pfalz, Ger.

59 Anna Gertraud [UNKNOWN], b. in Germany, d. in Hochstenbac, Pfalz, Ger.

4TH GREAT GRANDPARENTS

68 Patrick DYER, b. 1680, d. 1720 in Prince George's, MD, m. 12 Oct 1702 in Prince George's, MD.

69 Constant BARNES, b. 1685, d. Sep 1760 in Prince George's, MD.

112 Hans Jacob SCHMIDGEN, b. in Germany, d. 1707 in Hochstenbac, Pfalz, Ger., m. 1678 in Hochstenbac, Pfalz, Ger.

113 Anna Gertraut [UNKNOWN], b. in Germany, d. in Hochstenbac, Pfalz, Ger.

114 Hans Henrich VOHL, b. in Germany, d. 18 Jun 1714 in Hochstenbac, Pfalz, Ger., m. 29 Oct 1679 in Hochstenbac, Pfalz, Ger.

115 Eva Veronica [UNKNOWN], b. in Germany, d. 8 Jun 1728 in Hochstenbac, Pfalz, Ger.

---

40. **Thomas Lee^3 TURNER** (John Meredith, 7). Born, 10 Jul 1840, in Licking, OH. Died, 12 Sep 1916, in Clackamas, OR, age 76.[46]

He married Nancy Elizabeth POWER, daughter of Benjamin POWER and Hannah EVICK, 4 Apr 1861, in Adair, MO. Born, 19 Sep 1844, in MO. Died, 19 Jan 1911, in Clackamas, OR, age 66.[47] They were both buried at the Bird Cemetery in Stafford. They were on the 1870 to 1910 census for Tualatin, Clackamas, OR. In 1910 it was reported that they had been married 49 years, had 11 children, 10 of whom were still living.

"Our subject's father, John M. TURNER, was born in Virginia, reared to manhood there, and in that State married Miss Harriett COOK, and after their marriage they removed to Ohio and settled on a farm. In the fall of 1851 they moved to Missouri, purchased land and established their home on it. There the father resided till the time of his death, which occurred in 1857. In religion he was a Baptist, and in politics a Democrat. He was a soldier in the war of 1812. His widow survived him till 1885, being seventy-three years old at the time of her death. They were the parents of ten children, nine of whom reached adult years, and six are still living. Thomas L. is the youngest in this family, and was only thirteen years of age when his father died. He remained with his mother on the farm and aided her in the management of it until he grew up to manhood, and in due time he purchased land for himself."

"April 4, 1861, Mr. TURNER married, Miss Nancy POWERS... They remained on the farm until 1865, and that year crossed the plains to Oregon. They had three children born in Missouri... These children they brought with them across the plains, being six months on their journey, and, upon their arrival in Oregon, came direct to the farm on which they have since resided, seven miles northeast of Oregon City. They purchased 160 acres of land, at $2.50 per acre, paying $500 down and going in debt for the rest, and in a log house on this farm they began their pioneer life in Oregon. As the years rolled by their honest industry was crowned with success. In 1869 a good frame residence took the place of their primitive log house, and Mr. TURNER not only paid for his first purchase of land but also added 300 acres more to it, making 460 altogether."[48] Children:[49]

+	135	i.	Mary Frances[4] TURNER.
+	136	ii.	Julia Elizabeth TURNER.
+	137	iii.	John Marion TURNER.
	138	iv.	Anna M. TURNER. Born, 24 Nov 1868, in Clackamas, OR. Died, 19 Jun 1871, in Clackamas, OR, age 2. Buried at the Bird Cemetery.
+	139	v.	James Arthur. TURNER.
+	140	vi.	Albert F. TURNER.
+	141	vii.	Ella Harriet TURNER.
+	142	viii.	Herbert T. TURNER.
+	143	ix.	Lilley "Susie" TURNER.
+	144	x.	Charles E. TURNER.
+	145	xi.	Smith TURNER.

NOTES: CHAPTER 3 - THIRD GENERATION

[1] Scotland County, Missouri Land Patents 15583, 21803.

[2] Scotland County, Missouri Land Patents 20457, 20707, 21801, 21802.

[3] Scotland County, Missouri Land Patents 20151, 20706, 20933.

[4] Scotland County, Missouri Land Warrant 47.257.

[5] The land he received was in exchange for the surrendered Bounty Land Warrant #9919 issued 17 June 1851 by the U. S. Government. The application is at the National Archives in Washington, D.C., and the warrant is at the Archives Record Center in Suitland, MD.

[6] Bounty Land Warrant #24,380 issued 23 Oct 1855 by the U. S. Government. The application (#62956) is at the National Archives in Washington, D.C., and the warrant is at the Archives Record Center in Suitland, MD.

[7] Scotland County, Missouri Deeds, 53:442-447.

[8] Martin, *Martin Family History*, Ohio and Missouri chapters.

[9] Walter Williams, *History of Northeast Missouri*, 3 vols. (Chicago: Lewis Pub., Co., 1913), I:58-65.

[10] Confederate Service Records, Washington, DC, National Archives.

[11] *Biographical History of Crawford, Ida and Sac Counties, Iowa* (Chicago: Lewis Pub. Co., 1893), pp. 396-397.

[12] "Civil War and Later Series," Index Cards, National Archives, Microfilm T288, Roll #104.

[13] Ewing, *My Turner Family*, p. 17.

[14] Vogt & Kethley, *Shenandoah Marriage Bonds*, p. 214.

[15] *Biographical History of Crawford, Ida and Sac Counties, Iowa*, pp. 396-397.

[16] *Columbia County News*, 30 June 1909, Obituary.

[17] Obituary from unknown newspaper.

[18] *Columbia County News*, 7 April 1909, Obituary.

[19] Frank T. Gilbert, *Historic Sketches of Walla Walla, Whitman, Columbia and Garfield Counties, Washington Territory* (Portland, OR: A.G. Walling, 1882), p. 53 of appendix.

[20] Scotland County, Missouri Land Patents 26956, 26958, 17831.

[21] Ewing, *My Turner Family*, source not given.

[22] The published transcription of the cemetery records says 1881, but Dave MARTIN read the tombstone as 1891.

[23] Licking County, Ohio marriages, p. 464. Film #384,300.

[24] His tombstone is illegible. He deeded his property to Emeline MARTIN, 6 Nov 1895. Scotland County, Missouri Deeds, 56:96.

[25] Scotland County, Missouri Land Patent, 26974 (53:447); Scotland County, Missouri Deeds, C:72.
[26] For a complete family history, see Martin, *Martin Family History.*
[27] *Columbia County News*, September 1905.
[28] Muskingum County, Ohio Marriages. Film #317,459.
[29] Scotland County, Missouri Deeds, 53:443; Scotland County, Missouri Land Patent, 29444.
[30] *Biographical and Historical Memoirs of Muskingum County, Ohio* (Chicago: Goodspeed Pub. Co., 1892), p. 548.
[31] *Columbia County News*, 23 March 1895, 6 April 1895.
[32] Ward Rinehart, *Covello: A Pioneer Remembers* (College Place, WA: 1975), p. 89.
[33] He is listed in, Ewing, *My Turner Family*, p. E, but no record was found of him in the census. He may be the same as William A. born 1866.
[34] Washington State Death Index.
[35] Scotland County, Missouri Deeds, C:581.
[36] For a complete family history see, Martin, *Martin Family History*; Knox County, Missouri Probate Book, 1:99, dated 20 Jan 1879.
[37] Rinehart, *Covello*, pp. 84-85.
[38] W. F. Fletcher, *Early Columbia County* (Fairfield, WA: Ye Galleon Press, 1988), pp. 26-27.
[39] Knox County, Missouri Probate Book 1:99.
[40] Determining a middle name for this man has been difficult. His mother signed over Bounty Land Warrant #24,380 issued 23 Oct 1855 to John M. TURNER. His descendant, Norma BROOKS, Rt. 3 Box 372, Longview, TX 75603 gives him the middle initial "D." On most records he is just John TURNER.
[41] *Columbia County News*, 22 April 1899.
[42] William Denison Lyman, *Lyman's History of Old Walla Walla County* ... (Chicago: S. J. Clarke Pub. Co., 1918), pp. 721-722.
[43] Van Buren County, Iowa Circuit Court Administrator's Petition dated 18 Sep 1878 and Inventory dated 24 Dec 1887.
[44] Charles TURNER, Pvt., Capt. David W. CRAIG'S Co., SNIDER'S Batt'n, Northeast Missouri Cavalry Volunteers. Age 27 years. "The men are all mounted on good horses & most of them armed well." National Archives, Confederate Service Records.
[45] Clackamas County, Oregon, Marriages, 2:96.
[46] Oregon Death Index 1903-1921, Film #1,373,870.
[47] Oregon Death Index 1903-1921, Film #1,373,870.
[48] H. K. Hines, *An Illustrated History of the State of Oregon* (Chicago: Lewis Pub. Co., 1893), p. 1241.
[49] Information from Kae FLETCHER, Rt. 3 Box 302, Dayton, WA 99328, 4 Dec 1993.

CHAPTER 4

THE FOURTH GENERATION

The fourth generation of the children of John Meridy TURNER(1) were born in Virginia, Ohio, Missouri, Oregon and Washington. They died in Missouri, Iowa, Indiana, Oregon and Washington. From this we can see that the family was moving west. They were not frontier dwellers, but always moved after the area was settled, but still open for advancement. They were a conservative family that helped populate this country with steady, reliable people.

There was still a part of the TURNER family that remained in Missouri after the Civil War. But this great turmoil had caused many to seek another place to live where they could live in peace. In the summer of 1865, the three sons of John Meredith TURNER, John D.(38), Charles Daniel(39) and Thomas Lee(40) and the one son of Daniel Meridy TURNER, James Daniel(20) left Missouri for Oregon. John D. TURNER and James Daniel TURNER went to Yamhill County. Charles and Thomas settled in Clackamas County.

Only Thomas Lee TURNER remained in Oregon. The other three left Oregon for Walla Walla County in the Washington Territory. In March of 1871 John D. TURNER took up his abode on Whiskey Creek, in what became Columbia County in 1875. James Daniel TURNER homesteaded near Alto in the same year. Charles Daniel TURNER joined them and homesteaded near Huntsville about 1875. Public land was taken up under the preemption Act of 1841, under which a settler could claim and purchase up to 160 acres for $1.25 an acre or under the Homestead Act of 1862 where a citizen could claim title to 160 acres, provided he or she resided on the land for five years, made improvements, and paid a fee of $34.00. The Timber and Stone Act of 1878 set a fee of $2.50 an acre.[1]

It seems obvious from reading the history of the Columbia Basin area that there were many who settled here after the Civil War who were like-minded supporters of the Confederacy. The little town of Dixie just south of Waitsburg was named for the KERSHAW brothers, known for their singing of the song "Dixie" as they crossed the prairies toward Oregon.[2] The father-in-law of Joseph Edgar FREEMAN(243) was a Confederate veteran from North Carolina. David RAMSAUR had settled near Waitsburg about 1895.[3] Recent settlers in Umatilla County in Oregon were primarily Confederate Missourians and the street names in Pendleton commemorated such people as LEE, BAUREGARD, Jeff DAVIS and Stonewall JACKSON.[4] The Ku Klux Klan was an active organization in Columbia County as late as 1923. There is a picture of about 300 men marching in the Dayton Days parade wearing their long white robes.[5]

By 1870 the upper Touchet River was lined with farms; at its junction with Coppei Creek. The first of the new agricultural towns, Waitsburg, now numbered 107 inhabitants, and the local mill was one of the leading flour exporters. Many of the best sites farther east along the Tucannon and Pataha Rivers were already taken. Walla Walla city had a population of 1,394 in 1870.[6]

The total number of inhabitants in Columbia County in 1878 (which then included Garfield and Asotin Counties) was 5,820, which made it the most densely populated county in the Washington Territory. Walla Walla County was a close second with 5,701 and King County was third with 5,443. Many of the earliest settlers had immediately prepared ground for grain, gardens and orchards. From the Assessor's books of 1878 we find that the total acreage of Columbia County was as follows: wheat 28,337, barley 4,260, oats 4,260, timothy 633, corn 555, orchards 496, potatoes 205, alfalfa 15, flax 14 and clover 3.[7]

The Nez Perce Indian War of 1877 gave all of the residents of the area some uneasy weeks; however, the principal source of the dispute was the Wallowa country of Eastern Oregon. The Bannock and Piute Indian War of 1878, while not directly affecting any of the southern tier of counties in the Washington Territory, created excitement in Columbia County. People were continually on the lookout for a new Indian scare.[8]

The legislature of 1878-79 enacted a law changing the boundary line between Walla Walla and Columbia Counties by adding to Walla Walla County, Township 8 North, Range 38 East. It included the upper Dry Creek, Coppei and Whiskey Creek area. This put some of our early TURNER families into Walla Walla County again, after three years of being a part of the new Columbia County.

In 1879 there was marked advancement in Columbia County. The harvest was plentiful, the county free from Indian troubles, and the population had increased by 1,074 people and was still the most populous County in the Territory. In 1874 the spur railroad from

Walla Walla to the Touchet River had been completed and by 1881 the railroad went from Dayton, Washington to The Dalles, and in 1882 on to Portland, Oregon. In 1901 Ben TURNER was responsible for getting the railroad from Dayton to his farm where he provided badly needed warehousing. The station was named TURNERVILLE and later just TURNER. A roadbed was made as far as Covello but the tracks were never laid, dooming that town to extinction.[9]

TURNER, WASHINGTON

MAP OF WASHINGTON AND OREGON

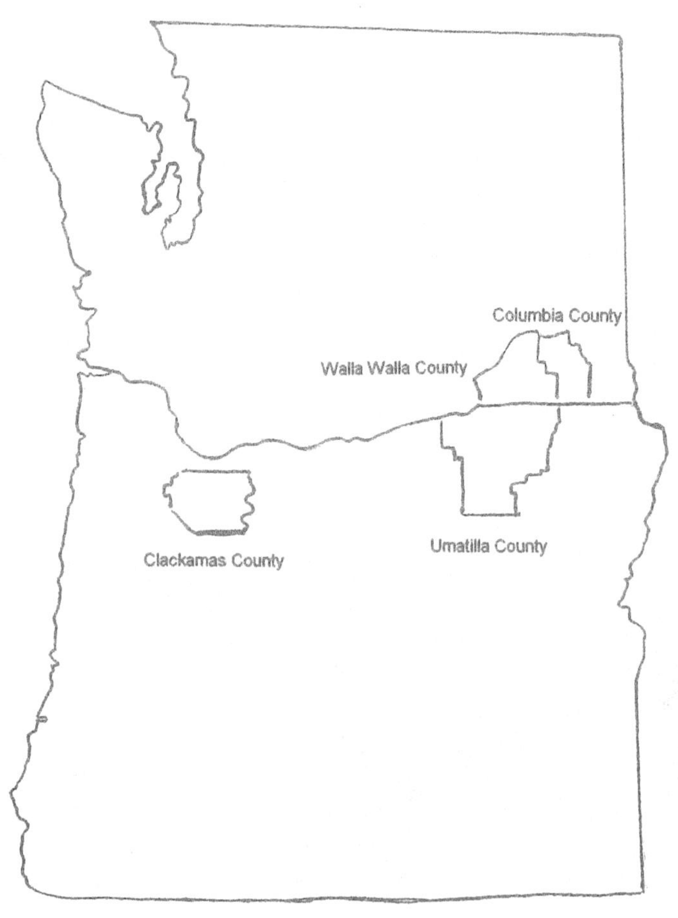

MAP OF OREGON COUNTIES

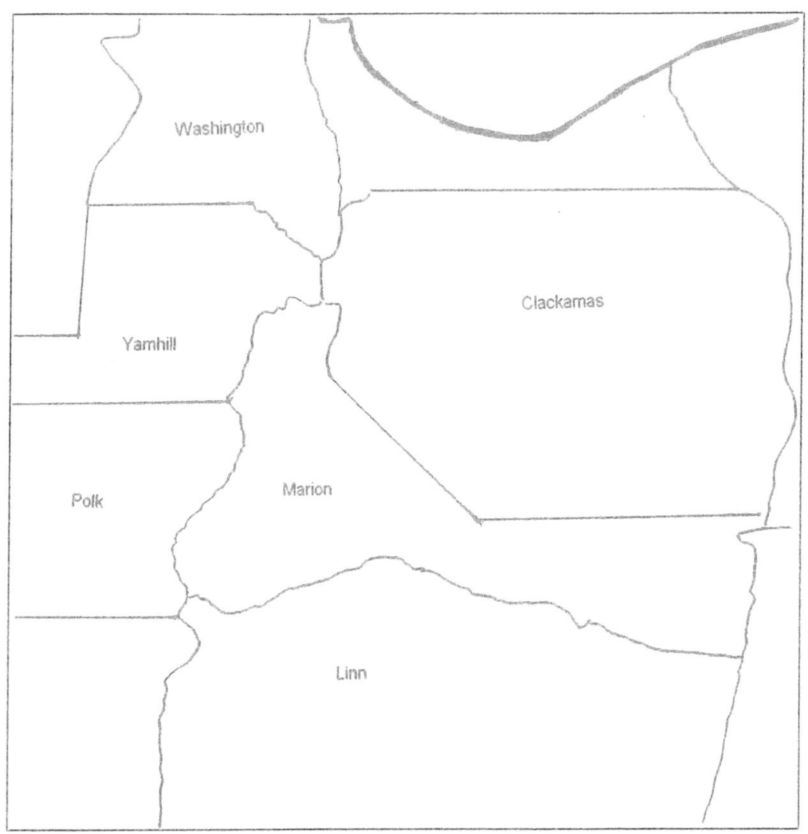

The first crossing of a family from the Missouri frontier overland to Oregon for the expressed purpose of settling and establishing a farm occured in 1840. The 1842 migration provided the nucleus of the frontier's first town, Oregon City. By 1847 the Great Migration had begun. Nearly 10,000 Americans had made their way to the Oregon Country. Most packed their belongings into covered wagons at Independence, Missouri, and crossed 2,000 miles of the continent to arrive six months later at the end of the Oregon Trail

In 1865 the three TURNER brothers and their first cousin, James Daniel, came to Oregon by wagon train. In 1870 Charles Daniel and Thomas Lee were living in Clackamas County. John D. was in Yamhill County and James Daniel was in Polk County.

MAP OF PROPERTY IN WASHINGTON

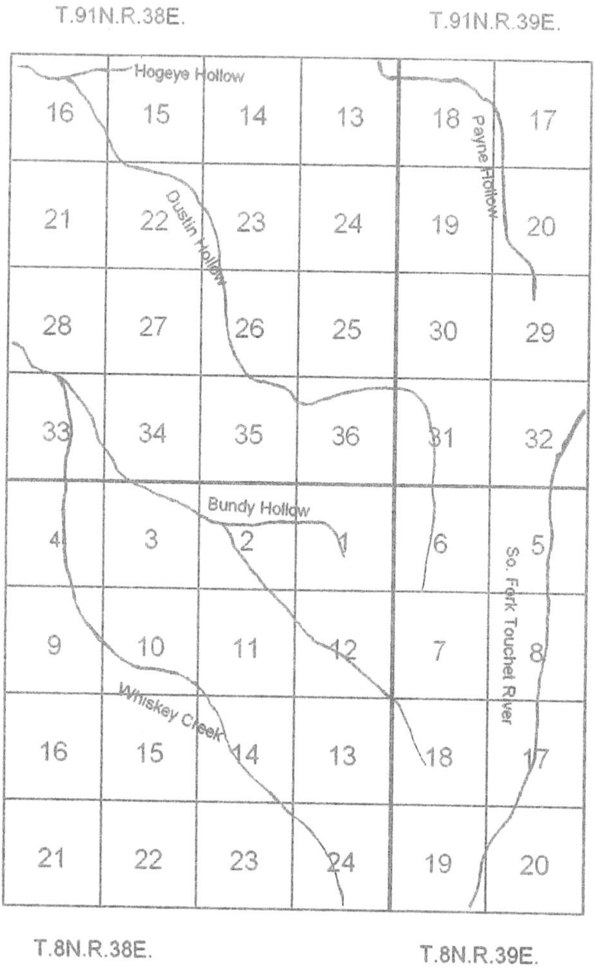

COLUMBIA COUNTY WASHINGTON
Land that was owned by members of the TURNER family.
Twp 8 Range 38 became a part of Walla Walla County in 1879.

Sources:

Homestead Act of June 3, 1878, National Archives, M1622, Film #36.

George A. Ogle, *Standard Atlas of Walla Walla County, Washington*, (Chicago, IL: George A. Ogle, 1909)

George A. Ogle, *Standard Atlas of Columbia County, Washington*, (Chicago, IL: George A. Ogle, 1913)

LAND RECORDS OF WASHINGTON

SECTION TOWNSHIP RANGE	ACRES	DATE	NAME
S21 T9N R38E	40A	1913	H. L. PRICE
S22 T9N R38E	80A	1913	H. L. PRICE
S24 T9N R38E	40A	4 May 1880	Chas. D. TURNER
S24 T9N R38E	160A	27 Oct 1876	Chas. D. TURNER
S25 T9N R38E	80A	5 Oct 1885	David TURNER
S25 T9N R38E	160A	28 Dec 1886	David TURNER
S26 T9N R38E	160A	5 Nov 1875	John TURNER
S27 T9N R38E	80A	Nov 1884	Jno. D. PRICE
		1913	H. L. PRICE
S27 T9N R38E	120A	1913	G. W. FREEMAN
S28 T9N R38E	80A	1913	G. W. FREEMAN
S28 T9N R38E	80A	Nov 1884	Jno. D. PRICE
	240A	1913	H. L. PRICE
S29 T9N R38E	160A	1913	G. W. FREEMAN
S29 T9N R38E	80A	Nov 1884	Jno. D. PRICE
		1913	H. L. PRICE
S30 T9N R38E	80A	Nov 1884	Jno. D. PRICE
S33 T9N R38E	160A	Dec 1886	James P. TURNER
S34 T9N R38E	160A	20 Oct 1877	Benj. M. TURNER
S35 T9N R38E	160A	4 Nov 1884	Francis M.WEATHERFORD
S18 T9N R39E	160A	27 Jan 1877	John D. PRICE
S19 T9N R39E	160A	28 Dec 1886	John B. REDFORD
		1913	J. B. & Amanda REDFORD
S20 T9N R39E	160A	28 Dec 1886	John B. REDFORD
		1913	E. L. LINDLEY lessee
S24 T9N R39E	160A	1913	J. PRICE
S25 T9N R39E	109A	1913	J. PRICE
S34 T9N R39E	40A	1913	M. M. TURNER
S 4 T8N R38E	120A	1909	J. D. PRICE
S 5 T8N R38E	161A	1909	Walter E. PRICE
S 5 T8N R38E	26A	1909	J. D. PRICE
S 8 T8N R38E	83A	1909	J. D. PRICE
S 9 T8N R38E	120A	1909	J. D. PRICE
S14 T8N R38E	40A	1 May 1879	James D. TURNER
S22 T8N R38E	160A	15 Dec 1879	Jno. M. TURNER
S 6 T8N R39E	40A	9 Mar 1880	Chas. D. TURNER
S 6 T8N R39E	39¼A	11 Mar 1880	John R. EVANS
S18 T8N R39E	49A	19 Feb 1880	John B. REDFORD
S19 T8N R39E	42A	17 Feb 1880	Benj. M. TURNER
		1913	J. D. PRICE

MAP OF PROPERTY IN WASHINGTON

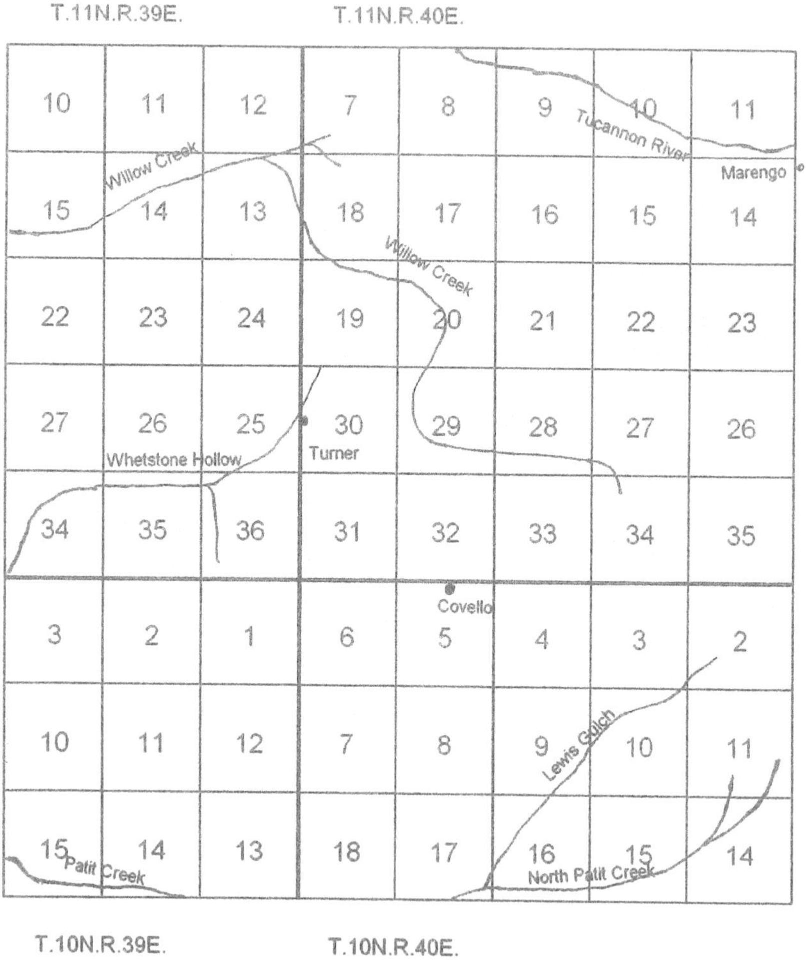

T.11N.R.39E. T.11N.R.40E.

10	11	12	7	8	9	10	11
15	14	13	18	17	16	15	14
22	23	24	19	20	21	22	23
27	26	25	30	29	28	27	26
34	35	36	31	32	33	34	35
3	2	1	6	5	4	3	2
10	11	12	7	8	9	10	11
15	14	13	18	17	16	15	14

Tucannon River
Marengo
Willow Creek
Willow Creek
Turner
Whetstone Hollow
Covello
Lewis Gulch
Patit Creek
North Patit Creek

T.10N.R.39E. T.10N.R.40E.

COLUMBIA COUNTY WASHINGTON
Land that was owned by members of the TURNER family.

Sources:

Homestead Act of June 3, 1878, National Archives, M1622, Film #36.

Ward Rinehart, *Covello: A Pioneer Remembers* (College Place, WA: 1975), "Land owners map 1900," between pp. 87 & 88.

George A. Ogle, *Standard Atlas of Columbia County, Washington*, (Chicago, IL: George A. Ogle, 1913)

LAND RECORDS OF WASHINGTON

SECTION TOWNSHIP RANGE	ACRES	DATE	NAME
S12 T11N R39E	160A	1913	C. O. JOHNSON
S13 T11N R39E	240A	1913	C. O. JOHNSON
S14 T11N R39E	320A	1900	Mary A. TURNER
		1913	James TURNER
S24 T11N R39E	240A	1900	J. S. MORRIS
		1913	C.W.&Melissa MORRIS
S24 T11N R39E	160A	1900 1913	B. M. TURNER
S25 T11N R39E	40A	1888	Jos. A TURNER
	320A	1900 1913	C. A. MARTIN
S26 T11N R39E	160A	1900	C. A. MARTIN
S34 T11N R39E	160A	1900	Henry MARTIN
	280A	1913	J. M. MARTIN
S36 T11N R39E	423A	1900	PRYOR Bros.
		1913	W. A. & C. W. PRYOR
S14 T11N R40E	80A	1913	J. A. ANDERSON
S19 T11N R40E	80A	1885	James P. TURNER
	640A	1900 1913	B. M. TURNER
S20 T11N R40E	320A	1900 1913	B. M. TURNER
S22 T11N R40E	240A	1900	J. A. ANDERSON
	400A	1913	O.V. ANDERSON lessee
S23 T11N R40E	80A	1913	J. A. ANDERSON
S27 T11N R40E	120A	1900 1913	J. A. ANDERSON
S30 T11N R40E	240A	1900 1913	B. M. TURNER
S30 T11N R40E		1913	Jos. TURNER
S31 T11N R40E	80A	1900 1913	C. W. PRYOR
S31 T11N R40E	80A	1900	W. A. PRYOR
		1913	C. W. PRYOR
S 3 T10N R39E	164A	1896	John D. MARTIN
		1900	John TURNER
S 3 T10N R39E	161A	1896 1900	John TURNER
S12 T10N R39E	320A	1913	F. M. WEATHERFORD
S22 T10N R39E	160A	1913	E. L. LINDLEY
S27 T10N R39E	80A	1913	E. L. LINDLEY
S 4 T10N R40E	200A	1900 1913	F. M. WEATHERFORD
S 5 T10N R40E	360A	1900	J. A. TURNER
		1913	Alexander PRICE Est.
S 6 T10N R40E	80A	1900 1913	C. W. PRYOR
S 7 T10N R40E	240A	1913	F. M. WEATHERFORD
S 8 T10N R40E	400A	1900 1913	F. M. WEATHERFORD
S 9 T10N R40E	160A	1900 1913	F. M. WEATHERFORD
S15 T10N R40E	280A	1913	C. A. MARTIN
S16 T10N R40E	78A	1913	C. A. MARTIN
S18 T10N R40E	160A	1913	F. M. WEATHERFORD

MAP OF COLUMBIA COUNTY, WASHINGTON

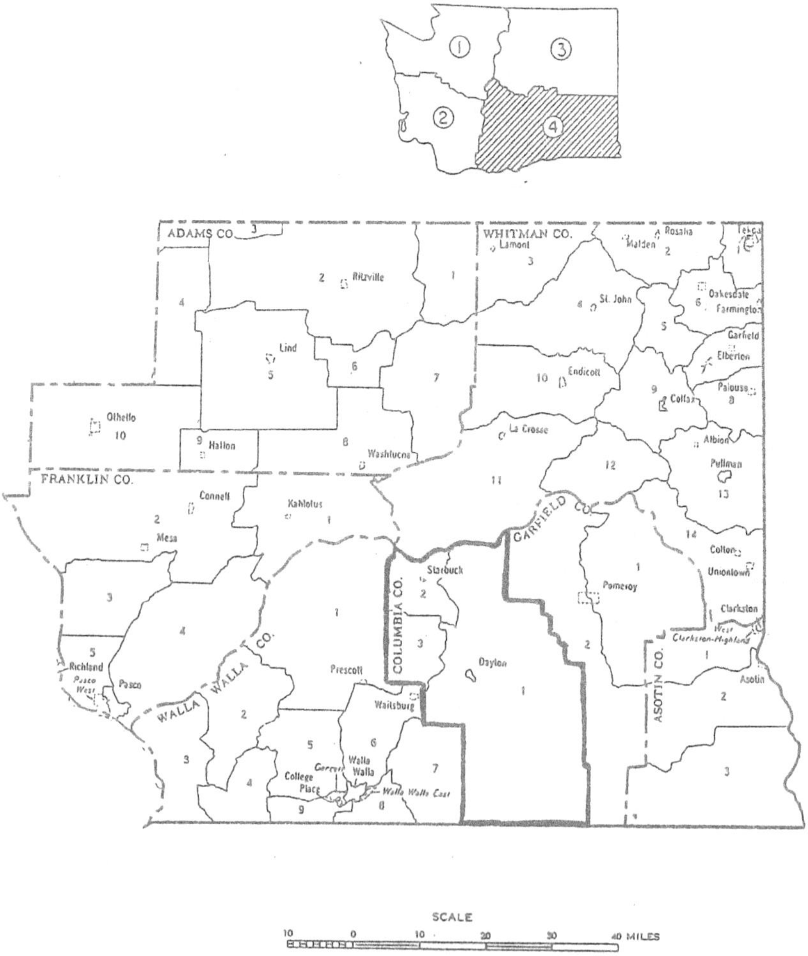

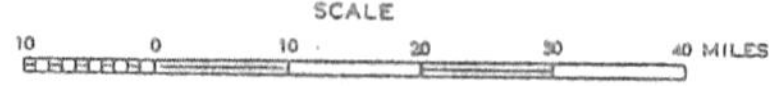

FOURTH GENERATION

41. **William A.^{4} TURNER** (William H., 13). Born, 1827, in VA. He had a patent for 40 acres of land in Section 11 dated 13 Oct 1853. Resided in Johnson Twp, Scotland, MO in the 1880 census.

He married Eliza Jane POWER, 26 Dec 1850, in Scotland, MO. Born, 1832, in IN. Children:

146 i. Charles T.^{5} TURNER. Born, 19 Aug 1851, in Scotland, MO. Died, 4 Sep 1864, in Scotland, MO, age 13. Buried in Power Cemetery.
147 ii. Bartlett TURNER. Born, 1852, in Scotland, MO. He married Mollie E. STANDARD, 26 Dec 1872, in Scotland, MO.
148 iii. John R. TURNER. Born, 7 Aug 1853, in Scotland, MO. Died, 23 Nov 1855, in Scotland, MO, age 2. Buried Power Cemetery.
149 iv. Lydia A. TURNER. Born, 1855, in Scotland, MO. She married Joseph A. WATERS, 2 Nov 1871, in Scotland, MO.
150 v. H. F. Born, 1855, in Scotland, MO. Died in Scotland, MO. Buried Power Cemetery. (Footstone marked H. F. T. with no dates.)
151 vi. James B. TURNER. Born, 9 Sep 1856, in Scotland, MO. Died in Scotland, MO. He married Julia ADAMS, 4 Feb 1875, in Scotland, MO. She d. 25 Dec 1889. Both buried in Black Oak Cemetery, near Granger.
152 vii. William TURNER. Born, 1859, in Scotland, MO.
153 viii. Oscar TURNER. Born, 1867, in Scotland, MO.

46. **James T.^{4} TURNER** (Alexander S., 16). Born, 9 Oct 1840, in Scotland, MO. Died, 13 May 1907, in Crawford, IA, age 66. Buried Deloit Cemetery.

He married Sarah Katharine CHILDERS, daughter of John M. and Nancy CHILDERS, 16 Jun 1861, in Fairmont, Clark, MO. Born, 1844, in MO. They are on the 1880 census in Stockholm, Crawford, IA. He was on the 1900 Milford, Crawford, IA census with second wife Ann, born Jan 1846, in MO.

"He was a soldier in the late war, after which he lived in Hancock Co., IL, then at Henderson Co., same state and in 1871 came to this county [Crawford, IA]. He has a well-improved farm of 86 acres with a good comfortable cottage and a fine grove and orchard... In his political views our subject is a Democrat and has held Justice of the Peace offices. He is a pastor of the Reorganized Church of Latter Day Saints of Deloit, an active worker in the cause. He has the respect and confidence of all who know him."[10] Children:

+ 154 i. Viola[5] TURNER.
+ 155 ii. Edwin TURNER.
156 iii. Mary Addie TURNER. Born, 1868, in AR. She married [Unknown] RAYMOND. Living in Marion, KS in 1893.
157 iv. Maude TURNER. Born, 25 Jun 1870, in Henderson, IL. Died, 1889, in Crawford, IA, age 19. She was a teacher.
158 v. Winnie TURNER. Born, Jul 1872, in Crawford, IA. She married Stanley BROWN in Deloit, Crawford, IA. He was born, Sep 1867, in NY. They were on the 1900 Milford, Crawford, IA census.
159 vi. Pleasant TURNER. Born, 25 Mar 1873, in Crawford, IA.
160 vii. Grace TURNER. Born, 1874, in Crawford, IA. She married [Unknown] MCMILLAN. Living in Sac, IA in 1893.
161 viii. James TURNER. Born, Jan 1876, in Crawford, IA. He married Ida [UNKNOWN], before 1900, in Crawford, IA. She was born, Oct 1877, in MI. They were on the 1900 Milford Twp, Crawford, IA census.
162 ix. Katy TURNER. Born, 1879, in Crawford, IA.
+ 163 x. Milliard J. TURNER.

47. **Mary Frances[4] TURNER** (Alexander S., 16). Born, 28 Dec 1843, in Scotland, MO. Died, 3 Jul 1902, in Enid, Garfield, OK, age 58.

She married Joseph R. GREGG, 1863, in Etna, MO. Born, Apr 1841, KY. They lived in Henderson, IL in 1865 and moved to Enid, OK in Nov 1901. They are on the 1900 census in Wyaconda, Clark, MO where his occupation was listed as produce shipper. Children:

164 i. Robert L.[5] GREGG. Born, 1867, in Henderson, IL.
165 ii. Elizabeth "Dollie" GREGG. Born, Feb 1869, in Henderson, IL. On the 1900 census she was living with her parents and was a school teacher. Clark, MO newspaper item dated 19 Jul 1901, "only Clark County lady thus far reported to try for land in Oklahoma."[11]

48. **Martha Ann[4] TURNER** (Alexander S., 16). Born, 10 Mar 1848, in Scotland, MO. Died, 8 Feb 1888, in Clark, MO, age 39. Buried in the Fairmont Cemetery.

She married Francis Marion ANDERSON, 16 Mar 1871, in Clark, MO. Born, Apr 1846, IN. They are on the 1880, Washington, Clark, MO census. He, along with his two daughters, is on the 1900 census in Wyaconda, Clark, MO as a widower employed as a stock shipper. Children:

166 i. Leona F.[5] ANDERSON Born, 1 Aug 1875, in Clark, MO. Died, 5 Aug 1877, in Clark, MO, age 2. Buried in the Fairmont Cemetery.
167 ii. Emma Bell ANDERSON. Born, Mar 1878, Clark, MO. She married Orval CURRIER.
168 iii. Mary A. ANDERSON. Born, 3 Apr 1881, in Clark, MO. Died, 19 Dec 1903, in Clark, MO, age 22. Buried in the Wyaconda Cemetery.

49. **John Alexander[4] TURNER** (Alexander S., 16). Born, 28 Feb 1850, in Scotland, MO. Died, 18 Oct 1931, in Clark, MO, age 81. Buried in the Wyaconda Cemetery.

He married Dora Alice GOLDSMITH, 13 Sep 1868, in Clark, MO. Born, 26 Feb 1853, in KY. Died, 23 Dec 1937, in Clark, MO, age 84. Both are buried in the Wyaconda Cemetery. They are on the 1880, 1900 1910 and 1920 Clark, MO census living in Washington township where his occupation is listed as farmer. Children:

\+ 169 i. William H.[5] TURNER.
\+ 170 ii. Florence G. "Jennie" TURNER.
171 iii. John Claude TURNER. Born, Jun 1874, in Clark, MO. Died, in CO. He married Lou E. ALLEN after 1900 when he was living with his father in Clark,

MO. Born, 1876. Died, 1916, age 40.[12]

- \+ 172 iv. Thadius TURNER.
- \+ 173 v. Nellie E. TURNER.
- 174 vi. Cecil TURNER. Born, 5 Sep 1884, in Clark, MO. Died, 12 Oct 1963, in Clark, MO, age 79. Buried in the Wyaconda Cemetery.
- \+ 175 vii. Lottie Gertrude TURNER.

50. **Nancy L.^{4} TURNER** (Alexander S., 16). Born, 15 Mar 1854, in Scotland, MO. Died, 23 Jan 1901, in Clark, MO, age 46. Buried in the Wyaconda Cemetery.

She married John P. GUSTIN, 31 Dec 1873, in MO. Born, Mar 1849, OH.They are on the 1900 census in Wyaconda, Clark, MO living on Jefferson Street where he was a hardware merchant. They are living with their daughter and her husband. Children:

- 176 i. John^5 GUSTIN.
- 177 ii. Nancy GUSTIN. Born, Mar 1875. She married Charles W. LANGRIDGE, 1897. Born, Feb 1868, VA. His occupation in 1900 was City Marshall.

53. **Mary M.^{4} TURNER** (Lewis, 18). Born, 22 Jan 1844, in MO. Died, 9 Oct 1906, in MO, age 62. Buried in the Wyaconda Cemetery.

She married Henry SMULLING, 23 Mar 1876, in Scotland, MO. Born, 1844, in IL. They were on the 1880 census living at Fairmont, Washington, Clark, MO. He had been married before and had children: Arther, Lafe, Amus, Nancy, and Mary E. Their children are named as Town age 2 and Jake age 7/12. Mary's sister, Demarus TURNER, is living with them. Children:

- 178 i. Stella Mahala^5 SMULLING. Born, 25 May 1877, in Knox, MO. Died, 15 Sep 1877.
- 179 ii. Thaddeus Wellington SMULLING. Born, 29 Jul 1878, in Clark, MO.
- 180 iii. Ray Walton SMULLING. Born, 29 Oct 1879, in Clark, MO. Died, 2 Oct 1911, in Hamilton, IL, age 31. He married Eliza MOTT, 24 Dec 1898, in Wyaconda, Clark, MO.
- 181 iv. William Elmer SMULLING. Born, 20 Nov 1881, in Clark, MO.

57. **Andrew Jackson[4] TURNER** (Lewis, 18). Born, 24 Mar 1854, in MO. Died, 27 Mar 1877, in MO, age 23. Buried Harmony Grove Cemetery.

He married Elizabeth V. SNIVELEY. Born, 1848, in MO. On the 1880 Wyaconda, Clark, MO census Elizabeth and her daughter, Fanny B. age 4 were living with Jacob RENCH. Child:

\+ 182 i. Frankie[5] TURNER.

She married, second, 27 Oct 1887, E. H. WILCOX, Scotland, MO.

67. **Mary Elizabeth[4] TURNER** (James Daniel, 20). Born, 5 Feb 1848, in Clark, MO. Died, 12 Mar 1923, Pilot Rock, Umatilla, OR, age 75.

She married John L. PRICE, son of William and Nancy PRICE, 17 Oct 1866, in Yamhill, OR. Born, 3 May 1842, in KY. Died, 17 Jul 1895, in Adams, Umatilla, OR, age 53. Buried in the Kees Cemetery near Weston, Umatilla, OR. They were on the 1870 Yamhill, OR census and the 1880 - 1920 Umatilla, OR census. In 1900 and 1910 they were in Adams precinct. Mary was living with her sons, Roy John and Earnest PRICE and grandson Leo B. PRICE [age 15], in the 1920 census in Pilot Rock.

"Mary Elizabeth TURNER was born in Scotland County, Missouri, on February 5, 1848 and died March 12, 1923 at the age of 75 years, 1 month and 17 days. She crossed the plains with her parents in 1865 to the Willamette Valley from Missouri, with ox teams. She was married to J. T. PRICE of Yamhill County, near McMinnville, on October 18, 1866. To this union were born eight children, five boys and three girls, four of whom have passed away, the husband also having died July 17, 1895. Those left to mourn her loss are Walter D. PRICE of Green Acres, Wash., Mrs. Frank LIEULLAN of Heppner, Ernest and Roy PRICE, of Pilot Rock also four sisters; Mrs. Jane WALLAN, of Adams, Oregon, Mrs. Amanda REDFORD, Mrs. Sidney LUCKINBEAL, and Mrs. Anna LINDLEY all of Dayton, Wash. and 14 grandchildren, 1 great-grandchild."[13] Children:

183 i. James W. PRICE. Born, 5 Jul 1870, in OR. Died, 13 Aug 1875, Umatilla, OR, age 5. Buried in the Kees Cemetery near Weston.

184 ii. Sarah Jane PRICE. Born, 8 Nov 1872, in OR. Died, 14 Nov 1872, Umatilla, OR. Buried in the Kees Cemetery near Weston.

185 iii. Thomas L.[5] PRICE. Born, Mar 1874, in OR. Died, before 1920. Buried in the Kees Cemetery near Weston, Umatilla, OR.

186 iv. Walter D. PRICE. Born, Jun 1879, in OR. He married Fern [UNKNOWN], c1912. Born, 1886, MI. They were on the 1920 census in Greenacres, Spokane, WA with three children.

187 v. Earnest A. PRICE. Born, Aug 1884, in Umatilla, OR.

188 vi. Amanda C. PRICE. Born, Oct 1886, in Umatilla, OR. She married Frank LIEUALLEN. He died, 9 Nov 1932, Umatilla, OR.[14]

189 vii. Roy John PRICE. Born, Dec 1888, in Umatilla, OR.

69. **Jane A.[4] TURNER** (James Daniel, 20). Born, Sep 1852, in Clark, MO. Died, 11 Mar 1926, age 73.[15] On the 1920 Adams, Umatilla, OR census she was living with her son, Ralph A. WALLAN.

She married William P. WALLAN, 1871, in OR. Born, Jul 1837, in MO. Died, 8 May 1910, in Umatilla, OR, age 72.[16] Buried in the Athena Cemetery where the gravestone is inscribed 1838 - 1910. He had two children by a previous marriage, George L., born 1862 and Herman, born 1867. They were on the 1880, 1900 & 1910 Adams, Umatilla, OR census.

In 1882 they were living 4 miles west of Centerville in Umatilla County where W. P. WALLAN was a farmer and mechanic and owned 160 acres. He was said to have been born in Jefferson, TN, 8 Feb 1857(sic), moved to Marion, OR in 1869 and to Umatilla, OR in 1879.[17] Children:

190 i. William D.[5] WALLAN. Born, Feb 1873, in OR.

191 ii. John F. WALLAN. Born, May 1876, in OR.

192 iii. M. Lottie WALLAN. Born, Jun 1880, in Umatilla, OR.

193 iv. Mary A. WALLAN. Born, Jul 1882, in Umatilla, OR.

194 v. Claude E. WALLAN. Born, Jan 1884, in Umatilla, OR.

195 vi. Edward C. WALLAN. Born, 27 Oct 1886, in

Umatilla, OR. Died, 24 Sep 1964, in Seattle, King, WA, age 77.[18]

196 vii. Clara E. WALLAN. Born, 1888, in Umatilla, OR.

197 viii. Grace O. WALLAN. Born, 1891, in Umatilla, OR. Died, 1897, Umatilla, OR, age 6. Buried at the Athena Cemetery.

198 ix. Ralph A. WALLAN. Born, 21 Nov 1894, in Umatilla, OR. Died, 7 Sep 1962, Umatilla, OR, age 67.[19] He married, Doris A. [UNKNOWN]. Born, 1901, IA. They were on the 1920 Umatilla, OR census.

70. **Sarah Elizabeth^4 TURNER** (James Daniel, 20). Born, 23 May 1857, in Scotland, MO. Died, 15 Nov 1916, in Kennewick, Benton, WA, age 59.[20] At the funeral of her father in 1909, she was reported as living in Wenatchee.

She married William Franklin ANDERSON, son of Thomas ANDERSON and Mary Ann POWER, 16 Jan 1873, at the residence of the bride's father near Waitsburg, Walla Walla, WA, by E. OLIVER, M.G. Born, 11 Apr 1848, in Scotland, MO. Died, 19 Dec 1928, in Spokane, Spokane, WA, age 80.[21] They were both buried in the Dayton Cemetery. In the 1900 census they were living in Stevens, WA.

A history of the first ferryman at Hunters was written by a grandson, T. Ross STATE in 1965, "Will Franklin ANDERSON and his family who came to the region from Dayton, Wash., in about 1895 or 1896 on the Stevens County shore of the Columbia River where he developed a farm and built and operated a cable ferry plying across the river to the Colville Indian Reservation. His farm site and ferry landing are now submerged by the back water of the Grand Coulee Dam, but the site of the present Camp Hunters recreational area park is either on or near a part of my grandfather's land... My grandfather and his family moved from this region in 1904 or 1905 to live in Wenatchee, Wash., leaving my father and our family to run the farm and operate the ferry."[22]

"Mrs. Sarah Louisa ANDERSON, wife of W. F. ANDERSON, of Wenatchee died at Kennewick, Wednesday, November the 15th, after a long period of ill health. A year ago she was brought to this city in hope of benefiting her health and from here went to Kennewick. She was nearly 60 years of age and was a resident of this city for many years. She is survived by her husband and ten children, her mother Mrs. James TURNER of Dayton, a sister Mrs.

Amanda REDFORD also of this city and other more distant relatives. The funeral will be held Sunday afternoon at 2:30 o'clock from the Christian Church with Rev. J. E. SLIMP officiating."[23]

"William ANDERSON ... came to Oregon with his parents at an early age. He came to Washington in 1871 and settled on a farm on Thorn Hollow which was his home for many years. He had most recently been living in Wenatchee and at the time of his death he was visiting a daughter in Spokane. Mr. ANDERSON was a brother of the late Mrs. Alex PRICE of this county, and a brother-in-law of Mrs. J. B. REDFORD of this city. He was survived by five daughters, Mrs. Jennie STATE, Mrs. Vernon SPALINGER, Mrs. Henry COOPER, and Mrs. Bob MYERS all of Spokane, and Mrs. Laura DASHIELL of Oakland, Calif., and five sons, Jess ANDERSON of Wenatchee, Thomas ANDERSON of this city, Lee ANDERSON of Prosser, and John ANDERSON BOWMAN, the little adopted son of Mr. and Mrs. W. J. BOWMAN, of this city."[24] Children:

199 i. Thomas J.[5] ANDERSON. Born, Nov 1873, in Columbia, WA. Died, 21 Feb 1934, in Spokane, WA, age 60. Lived in Dayton in 1928.

200 ii. Jennie May ANDERSON. Born, 1876, in Columbia, WA. She married Albert A. STATE, 1 Jun 1898, in Walla Walla, WA, by J. S. ANDERSON, M.G.. Lived in Spokane in 1928.[25]

201 iii. Amanda O. ANDERSON. Born, 23 Aug 1878, in Columbia, WA. Died, 16 Aug 1880, in Columbia, WA, age 2. Buried at Bundy Cemetery.

202 iv. Laura ANDERSON. Born, Jun 1881, in Columbia, WA. She married Earnest DASHIELL. "Ernest built houses, also rafted logs on the Columbia." They lived in Stevens, WA, moved to Oregon about 1907, and lived in Oakland, CA. in 1928.[26]

203 v. Susie ANDERSON. Born, Nov 1883, in Columbia, WA. She married [Unknown] POOL. Died, before 1928.

204 vi. Mary ANDERSON. Born, Oct 1885, in Columbia, WA. She married Bob MEYERS. Lived in Spokane in 1928.

205 vii. Lucy M. ANDERSON. Born, Mar 1887, in Columbia, WA. Died, 11 Feb 1988, in Everett, Snohomish, WA, age 100. She married Henry COOPER. Born, 1881, in AR. Died, 1968 or 1969 in Spokane, Spokane, WA.[27] Lived in Spokane in 1920 and 1928.

206 viii. Wilford ANDERSON. Born, Jul 1889, in Colum-

bia, WA. Died, before 1928.

207 ix. Stella ANDERSON. Born, Mar 1893, in Columbia, WA. She married Vernon L. SPALINGER. Born, 1891, OR. Died, 26 Jun 1972, Spokane, Spokane, WA, age 80.[28] They were living in Spokane in 1920 and in 1928.

208 x. Jesse ANDERSON. Born, Oct 1894, in Columbia, WA. Died, 3 Feb 1988, Wenatchee, Chelan, WA, age 92.[29] Lived in Wenatchee, Chelan, WA in 1920 and in 1928.

209 xi. Edward Lee ANDERSON. Born, Sep 1896, in Columbia, WA. He married Doris ROMANE. Lived in Prosser in 1928.

74. **Sidney Bell[4] TURNER** (James Daniel, 20). Born, 28 Nov 1865, in Yamhill, OR. Died, 21 Aug 1943, in Dayton, Columbia, WA, age 77.[30]

She married Samuel A. LUKINBEAL, 18 Nov 1886, in Dayton, Columbia, WA. Born, 14 Dec 1862, in MN or IA. Died, 11 Aug 1907, in Walla Walla, WA. Both were buried at the Waitsburg 6th St. Cemetery. They are on the 1889 and 1900 Lost Springs, Columbia, WA census.

"Samuel LUKINBELL died at St. Mary's Hospital in Walla Walla on August 11, age 45 years, 7 months, 28 days, of strangulation of the bowels. The remains were brought home to this city. Internment was at the I.O.O.F. Cemetery in Waitsburg."[31] Children:

210 i. Anna Bertha[5] LUKINBEAL. Born, Jan 1888, in Columbia, WA. Died, 23 Jul 1961, in Columbia, WA, buried in Dayton, age 73. She married Thomas F. SHEA. Born, 29 Apr 1884. Died, Feb 1972, Dayton, Columbia, WA, age 87.[32] They were living in Dayton on 4th Street on the 1920 census.

211 ii. Ralph LUKINBEAL. Born, 19 Jun 1889, in Columbia, WA. Died, 18 Jul 1969, in Walla Walla, buried in Dayton, Columbia, WA, age 80.[33] He married Viola M. STIMMEL. Born, 9 Feb 1890. Died, Mar 1963, Dayton, Columbia, WA, age 73.[34] They were living in Walla Walla on the 1920 census.

212 iii. Elbert LUKINBEAL. Born, Apr 1892, in Columbia, WA. Died, 24 Mar 1981, Dayton, Columbia, WA, age 88.[35] He was living with his mother on the

1920 census in Dayton, on Fremont Street.

76. **Mary "Emma"4 TURNER** (James Daniel, 20). Born, 26 Feb 1871, in Yamhill, OR. Died, 23 Sep 1901, Waitsburg, Walla Walla, WA, age 30.[36]

She married Conway D. DIXON, 26 Feb 1891, at the residence of J. B. REDFORD in Dayton, Columbia, WA. Born, Apr 1865, in MO. They are on the 1900 Waitsburg, Walla Walla, WA census. Children:

213 i. Bessie M.5 DIXON. Born, Sep 1892, in Waitsburg, Walla Walla, WA. Died, 16 Oct 1974, Walla Walla, WA, age 83.[37] Married Thaddeus C. STEVENS, circa 1915, in WA. Born, 1886, IA. They were on the 1920 census in Walla Walla living at 1322 Alder St.

214 ii. Delphia N. DIXON. Born, Jul 1894, in Waitsburg, Walla Walla, WA. Married [Unknown] HART.

215 iii. Alma Pearl DIXON. Born, 25 Aug 1895, in Waitsburg, Walla Walla, WA. Married [Unknown] FARRELL. Died, 8 Jul 1984, in Ellensburg, Kittitas, WA, age 88.[38]

77. **Anna Bertha4 TURNER** (James Daniel, 20). Born, 8 Jan 1876, near Waitsburg, Walla Walla, WA. Died, 1 Apr 1962, in Dayton, Columbia, WA, age 86.

She married Edward Lee LINDLEY, son of Levi LINDLEY and Susanna GAINES THOMPSON, 26 Nov 1893, at the bride's parents on South Touchet in Columbia, WA. Born, 22 Apr 1872, in Multnomah, OR. Died, 26 Apr 1930, in Dayton, Columbia, WA, age 58. Both were buried at the Dayton Cemetery. Children:[39]

216 i. Troy Tisdale5 LINDLEY. Born, 6 Oct 1894, in Columbia, WA. Died, 21 Dec 1965, in Escondido, San Diego, CA, age 71. He married Roberta HOUCHINS, daughter of James HOUCHINS and Margaret ROBERTS, 29 Dec 1920, in Waitsburg, Walla Walla, WA. In 1929 he was elected first president of the Columbia County Grain Growers, Inc.[40]

217 ii. "Baby" LINDLEY. Born, 9 Feb 1898, in Columbia, WA. Died, 23 Mar 1898, in Columbia, WA.

218 iii. Emile Stanley LINDLEY. Born, 13 Sep 1899, in Columbia, WA. Died, Dec 1976, Portland, Multnomah, OR, age 77. He married Josephine HAMILTON, daughter of J. H. HAMILTON and Josephine NEILL, 3 Mar 1923, in Portland, Multnomah, OR. Born, 20 Sep 1902. Died, Aug 1983, Eugene, Lane, OR, age 80.[41]

219 iv. Susie Lucille LINDLEY. Born, 1 Sep 1902, in Columbia, WA. Died, 18 Oct 1902, in Columbia, WA.

220 v. Helen May LINDLEY. Born, 14 May 1905, in Columbia, WA. Died, 12 Dec 1970, Walla Walla, WA, buried Dayton, Columbia, WA, age 65. She married Denver HENRY, son of Sam HENRY, 7 Jan 1945, in Columbia, WA.[42] Born, 17 Dec 1900. Died, 12 Aug 1976, Walla Walla, WA, buried Dayton, Columbia, WA, age 75.[43]

221 vi. Leo Byron LINDLEY. Born, 20 Sep 1909, in Columbia, WA. Died, 28 Nov 1973, in Walla Walla, buried in Dayton, Columbia, WA, age 64.[44]

222 vii. Jasper Lawson LINDLEY. Born, 27 Jul 1912, in Columbia, WA. Died, 10 Aug 1914, in Columbia, WA.

223 viii. Hazel Margaret LINDLEY. Born, 31 Jul 1915, in Columbia, WA. Died, 13 Jul 1967, in Portland, Multnomah, OR, age 51. She married Gilbert L. GILBREATH, son of Lee GILBREATH and Iona WHITE, 18 Oct 1939, in Dayton, Columbia, WA.

118. **Benjamin M.[4] TURNER** (John D., 38). Born, 15 Mar 1854, in Scotland, MO. Died, Sep 1934, in Columbia, WA, age 80.

He married, first, Samima J. BOYLES, 14 Oct 1876, in Columbia, WA. Born, 1859, TX. They are on the 1880, 1885, 1887 census of Columbia, WA. On the 1900 census Benjamin TURNER is listed as widowed.

He married, second, Anna BOROFSKY, Jan 1905, in Columbia, WA. The Columbia County News, 21 Jan 1905, reported that Anna was the eldest daughter of Mrs. VON CADOW. Her sister, Alma, was the bridesmaid and her brother John gave her away. Born, 1875. Died, 8 Jun 1943, age 68, Columbia, WA. They are both buried at the Dayton Cemetery.

"Ben M. TURNER is a self-made man of Columbia County who from pioneer times has been identified with the agricultural development and with kindred interests in southeastern Washington. Starting our empty-handed, he possessed energy and determination, together with a keen sagacity that has enabled him to recognize and utilize opportunities which others have passed heedlessly by. He now (1918) resides on section 19, township 11 north, range 40 east, in Columbia county, and has become well known as a farmer, as a breeder of Belgian horses and as a grain dealer and warehouseman.

Ben M. TURNER was educated in the district schools but his opportunities in that direction were quite limited. He was a youth of eleven years at the time of the emigration to the northwest and he became an active factor in assisting his father in the arduous task of developing and improving a new farm. Day after day saw him in the fields working to break the sod and cultivate crops, and on reaching his twenty-first year he began farming for himself. He purchased a quit claim to a preemption of 160 acres, on which he proved up, and with that tract as a beginning he had extended his farm holdings until he was one of the largest landowners of this section of the state.

Of recent years, however, he has disposed of all but two sections of land which is now being operated by tenants. He retired from active farming, although for many years he was extensively and successfully engaged in the tilling of the soil. He not only brought his fields under a high state of cultivation and demonstrated the possibility of producing fine crops in this section of the state but he also engaged in the breeding of Belgian horses. He secured two of the best mares in the northwest and his horses afterward received awards at the Washington State Fair at North Yakima, the Walla Walla Fair and the Cascade Stock Show at North Yakima. In fact he has won premiums on his stock at many fairs in the Northwest.

Since retiring from active farm work he has given his attention to the grain business and owns and operates an elevator at TURNER and is also in charge of the warehouses of the Portland Milling Company at TURNER, handling about two hundred and fifty thousand bushels of grain in 1916. He is thus connected with extensive and important business interests, which are carefully directed, for he is a man of sound judgment, keen discrimination and of unfaltering industry.

He belongs to Columbia Lodge, No. 26, F. & A. M., and Dayton Chapter, No. 5, R. A. M., and is a most worthy follower of the craft, exemplifying in his life its beneficent teachings concerning the brotherhood of mankind and the obligations thereby imposed. In politics he has always been a democrat but never has he sought public office, preferring to concentrate his energies and attention upon his business interests, which have gained him place among the most substantial citizens of southeastern Washington."[45]

He is listed in the 1913 Atlas as a Farmer, Stockraiser and Breeder of Registered Belgium Horses.[46]

Ward RINEHART says that B. M. TURNER "was a leader wherever he lived. He was largely responsible for the railroad extension to his farm and for Turnerville which followed. He provided badly needed warehousing. He was an active churchman, especially after retirement."[47]

RINEHART also told about his own father in relation to Ben TURNER. "Michael D. RINEHART came from Arkansas in 1883 as an orphan with two married brothers and a single one. He was thirteen when the emigrant train landed them in Walla Walla. He made an immediate hit with Uncle Ben TURNER for whom he worked his first year out West.

Years later Uncle Ben told me a story about my father I think is worth repeating here. There were seven hired men living at the TURNERS that winter. They slept in the runway between two wings of the barn with their blankets spread out on loose straw. They were all inclined to be somewhat slow in getting out of a morning when Uncle Ben called them at four and hung the lantern on the wall. Finally he said to young Mike, "You'll never amount to anything Mike, until you learn to get out of bed without delay when you're supposed to." Mike said he would sure like to but it took so long to come to he sometimes went back to sleep while he was trying to rouse himself. Uncle Ben said, "If you'll do what I tell you you'll never have any more trouble getting up. As soon as I call jump right out in the hay and start bucking like a horse on your hands and knees. Put all you've got into it."

So the next morning after Uncle Ben called the boys, he stepped out of sight to watch what happened. Sure enough Mike plunged from between the covers to the loose straw in one move and landed on all fours. He bucked and wheeled and got so enthused he began to roar like a bucking bronc. One by one the others followed suit. Uncle Ben said it was one of the funniest sights he ever witnessed seeing seven men bucking and bawling in the half light from the lantern. But they were all at breakfast for the first time all winter."[48]

119. **Samantha Ann^4 TURNER** (John D., 38). Born, Feb 1856, in Scotland, MO. Died, 25 Jan 1929, in Walla Walla, WA, age 72.[49]

She married John D. PRICE, son of Joseph Shores PRICE and Sarah WILLIAMS, 15 Feb 1872, by John M. HARRIS, Elder, at the residence of John TURNER, Walla Walla, WA. Witnesses were Leroy BROWN and James TURNER. Born, Jan 1849, in Knox, MO. Died, 1 Mar 1928, in Walla Walla, WA, age 79.[50] Both were buried at the Waitsburg Cemetery on 8th Street. They are on the 1889, 1900, census of Columbia County. However, he also owned land just over the line in S4 and S9 of T8N R38E in Walla Walla County in 1909.[51]

John D. PRICE and John L. PRICE(67) were first cousins. They are living near each other on the 1850 Knox, MO census when John D. was listed as age 1 and John L. was age 8. The brother of John D., Alexander PRICE, was living with John L. in the 1870 census in Yamhill, OR. Alexander PRICE married the half-sister of Samantha TURNER, Clarinda Jane ANDERSON, in 1873 in Walla Walla, WA. Clarinda was the sister of William ANDERSON who m. Sarah TURNER(70) who was the half-sister of Mary TURNER(67) the wife of John L. PRICE. Children:

224 i. Walter E.^{5} PRICE. Born, Feb 1874, in Walla Walla, WA. Died, 22 Apr 1949, Waitsburg, Walla Walla, WA, age 75. He married Ella E. MINNICK, 29 Nov 1899, by L. C. MARTIN, M.G., in Walla Walla, WA. Born, 1875. Died, 1 Mar 1963, Waitsburg, Walla Walla, WA, age 87. Both are buried at the Waitsburg City Cemetery. "Bundy Hollow: Walter PRICE & family spent Christmas [1906] with his brother, Harvey PRICE & family."[52] They lived on S5 T8N R38E, P.O. Waitsburg in 1909. He served as School Director for four years.[53] They were on the 1920 census at Walla Walla.

225 ii. Harvey Leander PRICE. Born, 27 Aug 1876, in Columbia, WA. Died, 27 Aug 1951, Waitsburg, Walla Walla, WA, age 75. He married Sarah Anna [UNKNOWN]. Born, 30 Jan 1880. Died 13 Dec 1926, Waitsburg, Walla Walla, WA, age 46. They are both buried at the Waitsburg I.O.O.F. Cemetery. "Bundy Hollow: Born on Thanksgiving Day [1907] a son to Mr. and Mrs. Harvey PRICE."[54] They are on the 1910 census at Bundy Precinct, Columbia, WA. He was School Director of School

District No. 12.[55]

226 iii. Annie PRICE. Born, 1 May 1889, Columbia, WA. Died, 26 Aug 1889, age 3 months.[56] Buried at the Waitsburg City Cemetery. She is on the 1889 census.

120. **Harriet Antoinette[4] TURNER** (John D., 38). Born, 27 Mar 1858, in Scotland, MO. Died, 25 Mar 1926, in Columbia, WA, age 67.[57]

She married Francis Marion WEATHERFORD, son of Alfred H. WEATHERFORD and Sophia SMITH, 5 Nov 1878, in Columbia, WA. Born, 12 Nov 1855, in Putnam, MO. Died, 4 May 1925, in Columbia, WA, age 69.[58] Both were buried in the Dayton Cemetery. They are on the 1887 Walla Walla, WA census; 1900 Covello, Columbia, WA census; 1910 Touchet, Columbia, WA census and the 1920 Dayton, Columbia, WA census. In 1920 a daughter-in-law Rose, a granddaughter Mary Belle, and a sister-in-law, Katherine TURNER, widow of Joseph TURNER(125), are living with them.

"Hon. F. M. WEATHERFORD is now living practically retired in Dayton but for many years was actively and extensively connected with farming interests and is still the owner of much valuable wheat land in this section of the state. Moreover, he has been prominently connected with public affairs and has been called upon to represent his district in the general assembly...

He crossed the plains in 1864, when a lad of but nine years, and became a resident of Linn county, Oregon. The trip was made with ox teams and wagon and he was six months en route... He took up his abode with a brother in Oregon and there remained until 1872, when he made his way northward to Walla Walla County, Washington. The following year, when a youth of eighteen, he rented a farm nine miles southwest of Dayton in the section known as Bundy Hollow. Later he bought land east of Dayton and occupied that farm for twenty years... He is now owner of sixteen hundred acres of fine wheat land in Columbia county.

He was also at one time vice president of the Farmers Exchange at Waitsburg, which he aided in organizing. He has now put aside the more active work of the fields, leaving that to others, while he is enjoying a well earned rest, having taken up his abode in Dayton. His farm property yields to him a most gratifying annual income and his energy and sound business judgment have brought him success. [His sons J. C. and Arthur M. were living on the home farm in 1918.]

In his political affiliation Mr. WEATHERFORD is a democrat and has taken an active part in advancing the interests of the organization. His fellow townsmen, appreciative of his worth and his devotion to the party, elected him to represent them for one term in the state legislature. The cause of education finds in him a stalwart champion and he has done effective work in behalf of the schools as a member of the school board. Fraternally he is connected with Dayton Lodge, No. 136, I. O. O. F., and both he and his wife are members of the Methodist Episcopal church, South, and in its work take an active and helpful interest, doing all in their power to extend its growth and promote its purpose."[59] Children:

227 i. William Meriday^5 WEATHERFORD. Born, 4 Oct 1879, in Columbia, WA. He married, Rose [UNKNOWN]. Died, 12 Nov 1918, in Columbia, WA, age 39.[60] Buried at Dayton Cemetery.

228 ii. James Clyde WEATHERFORD. Born, May 1882, in Columbia, WA. Died, 3 Jan 1956, Columbia, WA, age 73.[61] He married Fleta WARD in Columbia, WA. Born, 1887. Died, 23 May 1964, Columbia, WA, 78.[62] Both were buried in the Dayton Cemetery.

229 iii. Mary Susan WEATHERFORD. Born, Sep 1884, in Columbia, WA. Died, 2 Sep 1955, Columbia, WA, age 71.[63] She married Elmer F. DUNLAP. Born, 1887. Died, 22 Aug 1954, Columbia, WA, age 66.[64] Both were buried in the Dayton Cemetery where the monument gives her birth date as 1886.

230 iv. Clarabelle WEATHERFORD. Born, 11 Feb 1887, in Columbia, WA. Died, 10 Feb 1969, in Dayton, Columbia, WA, age 82.[65] She married W. Emory BRUCE.

231 v. Arthur M. WEATHERFORD. Born, 18 Jul 1890, in Columbia, WA. Died, 7 Mar 1967, in Toppenish, Yakima, WA, age 76.[66] He married Sadie THRONSON, daughter of C. J. THRONSON, circa 1916, in Dayton, Columbia, WA.[67] Born 10 Jun 1896. Died, 24 Apr 1969, Toppenish, Yakima, WA, age 72. Both were buried in the Dayton Cemetery.

121. **John Thomas⁴ TURNER** (John D., 38). Born, Jul 1860, in Adair, MO. Died, 2 Apr 1926, in Walla Walla, WA, age 66.[68] Buried at the Dayton Cemetery. He homesteaded on Willow Creek.[69]

He married S. Laura LAUGHERY, daughter of Robert LAUGHERY and Delila [UNKNOWN], 24 Dec 1883, in Dayton, Columbia, WA. Born, Jul 1867, in OR or WA. Died, 1923, age 56. They were divorced before the 1900 census when she was listed with her father and John T. TURNER was in Curlew, Ferry, WA. Children:[70]

+	232	i.	Grover Thomas[5] TURNER.
	233	ii.	Ora Robert TURNER. Born, 27 Dec 1886, in Columbia, WA. Died, 10 Oct 1887, in Columbia, WA. Buried at the Turner Cemetery.
+	234	iii.	Cora Irene TURNER.
+	235	iv.	Clarence Roy TURNER.

122. **James Patten[4] TURNER** (John D., 38). Born, 1862, in Adair, MO. Died, 1 Mar 1922, in Walla Walla, WA, age 59. Buried at the Waitsburg 8th Street Cemetery. It was reported in the *Columbia Chronicle* that Mr. and Mrs. B. M. TURNER came to Dayton from California several weeks before March 4, 1922 on account of the illness of James TURNER.[71]

He married Emma J. ATCHISON, 24 Jan 1884, in Columbia, WA. Born, Jun 1867, in WA. They were together on the 1885, 1887 and 1889 Columbia Co. territorial census. They were divorced.[72] Emma and the two children, George and Naomie, were on the 1900 census on Sprague Street in Spokane, WA. Children:

236	i.	Charles W.[5] TURNER. Born, 1885, in Columbia, WA. Died, 1886, in Columbia, WA. Buried in the Waitsburg Cemetery.
237	ii.	George F. TURNER. Born, Apr 1886, in Columbia, WA.
238	iii.	Silvy A. TURNER Born, 1888, in Columbia, WA. Died, 1889, in Columbia, WA. Buried in the Waitsburg Cemetery.
239	iv.	Naomie TURNER. Born, Dec 1891, in Columbia, WA.

123. **Joseph A.[4] TURNER** (John D., 38). Born, Aug 1865, on the Oregon Trail. Died, 3 Dec 1908, in Spokane, Spokane, WA, age 43.

His homestead bordered the town of Covello. Alexander PRICE later acquired the Joe TURNER holdings at Covello.[73]

"Mrs. F. M. WEATHERFORD returned from Spokane where her brother Joseph A. TURNER was seriously ill. The funeral will be held Sunday by the Masonic Order. He died at Deaconess Hospital, Spokane, age 43. Two years ago he moved to Oaksdale, Washington. He will be buried in the Dayton Cemetery. He leaves a wife, two sons, a daughter, mother and several brothers and sisters."[74]

He married Kate M. CROSS, 1888. Born, May 1868, in WA. Died, after 1920. The newspaper of 6 March 1909 reported that "Mrs. Joseph TURNER and son James arrived from Oaksdale to make this city their home."[75] They were on the 1889, and 1900 Columbia, WA census. On the 1910 Dayton census she was listed as a dressmaker. In 1920 she was living with her sister-in-law Harriet A. WEATHERFORD(120) in Dayton. Children:

240 i. Vizillia P.[5] TURNER. Born, Jan 1891, in Columbia, WA. On the 1910 Dayton census she was listed as a saleslady in a department store. She married [Unknown] JAMES.

241 ii. Benjamin "Clifford" TURNER. Born, Mar 1897, in Columbia, WA. He married Diehl H. [UNKNOWN], 1919, in Columbia, WA. Born, 1899, WI. They were on the 1920 census in Dayton.

242 iii. James M. TURNER. Born, Jan 1900, in Columbia, WA. He is on the 1920 census living as a roomer on Patit Ave with James A. MACLACHLAN.

126. **Sydney Irene[4] TURNER** (John D., 38). Born, 7 Feb 1869, in Yamhill, OR. Died, 9 Aug 1935, Waitsburg, Walla Walla, WA, age 66.

She married George Washington FREEMAN,[76] son of James Wesley FREEMAN and Sarah Caroline RIPLEY, 7 Jan 1886, in Walla Walla, WA, by Neal CHEETHAM, M.G., at the residence of John TURNER. Born, 24 Oct 1854, in Warrensburg, Johnson, MO. Died, 17 Sep 1943, in Waitsburg, Walla Walla, WA, age 88. They are both buried at the Waitsburg City Cemetery. They are on the 1889 Columbia, WA census and they lived at Waitsburg, Walla Walla, WA in 1900. On the 1920 census they are still living in Waitsburg on Coppei Avenue where George is listed as age 65 and Irene as age 50. Children:

243 i. Joseph Edgar^5 FREEMAN.[77] Born, 4 Mar 1887, in Columbia, WA. Died Aug 1955, San Ysidro, San Diego, CA, age 68. He married Winnie Davis RAMSAUR, daughter of David RAMSAUR, 4 Nov 1909, Walla Walla, WA. Born, 13 Feb 1891, Newton, Catawba, NC.

244 ii. George Earl FREEMAN. Born, 21 Mar 1896, in Columbia, WA. Died, 3 May 1964, in Waitsburg, Walla Walla, WA, age 68.[78] He is buried at the Waitsburg I.O.O.F. Cemetery. He married Niona STEVENS before the 1920 census when they are living in Columbia County. Born, 1900. Died, 4 Sep 1988, Dayton, Columbia, WA, age 88.[79]

125. **Charles M.^{4} TURNER** (John D., 38). Born, May 1872, in Walla Walla, WA. Died, 26 Nov 1942, in Stevens, WA, age 70.[80]

He married Agnes N. WALKER, daughter of James Theodore WALKER and Agnes MURRAY, before 1900, in WA. Born, Oct 1875, in VA. Died, 14 May 1959, age 83.[81] Both were buried in the Cedonia Cemetery. In the 1900 census they lived in Cedonia, Stevens, WA. In the 1920 census they were in Spokane.

"LOT 22 Charles and Agnes WALKER TURNER and their children, Mary and James are buried here. Mrs. TURNER was a nurse and midwife in the community, Sunday School teacher and known to the children and young people as "Auntie TURNER" and friend to all.

She was the daughter of James F. WALKER and Agnes MURRAY WALKER who came to the south fork of Harvey Creek in 1908. Later they lived south of Cedonia, just north of the grade on Highway 25 that bears their name. Mrs. TURNER was a sister to Edith COONEY, Everett WALKER, Lynn WALKER, and Grace and Florence IVEY.

Charlie was a great story teller and never expected people to believe all he said. They owned the Cedonia Store for a number of years, trading it to Mr. and Mrs. Rob DASHIELL sometime before 1916. In later years, they lived far up the north fork of Harvey Creek. Roy ENGLEHARDT owns the place now.

Many persons of my generation owe their safe advent into this world to Mrs. TURNER."[82] "Agnes WALKER TURNER became a favorite helper of Dr. Roderick D. MCRAE, going along to help in difficult cases. Many of the present residents of this section of Stevens County were ushered into the world by this famous pair.[83] Children:

245 i. Mary A.[5] TURNER. Born, 1904, in Cedonia, Stevens, WA. Died, 1919, age 15. Buried at the Cedonia Cemetery.

246 ii. James TURNER. "Son of C. M. and A. N. TURNER. Died Oct. 29, 1876 (sic) age 4 mo., 5 days."[84]

126. **Harriet Tabitha[4] TURNER** (Charles Daniel, 39). Born, 21 May 1858, in Knox, MO. Died, 19 Apr 1940, age 81, near Dayton, Columbia, WA, at the farm home of her daughter, Della JOHNSON.

She married Richard Henry BEEMAN, son of Rufus Horatio BEEMAN and Caroline MCBEE, 31 Mar 1880, in Dayton, Columbia, WA. Born, 20 Dec 1858, in Roseburg, Douglas, OR. Died, 5 Jul 1926, age 65, in Medical Lake, Spokane, WA. They were both buried at the Rose City Cemetery in Portland, OR, where their youngest daughter Almedia BOYER lived.

They are on the 1880 census in Columbia, WA but by 1881 they were in Nez Perce, ID where Henry BEEMAN'S parents were living. About 1895 they moved to Wallowa, OR where they homesteaded and had a sawmill on Trail Creek near the town of Imnaha. On the 1900 census they are in Pine Creek Precinct, Wallowa, OR with six children at home. They lived in Enterprise from 1913 to 1918 where they owned the hotel.

They then moved to Riverside, Okanogan, WA where they farmed and worked in the orchards. On the 1920 census they are living alone, both age 61, and he was farming. After Henry's death in 1926, Harriet lived with her children. Children:[85]

247 i. Alice Laverney[5] BEEMAN. Born, 13 Feb 1881, in Little Potlatch, Nez Perce, ID. Died, 3 Jul 1945, in Dayton, Columbia, WA, age 64. She married Cone Lucian JOHNSON, son of James W. JOHNSON and Samantha PATTERSON, 26 Mar 1899, in Dayton, Columbia, WA. Born, 5 Jan 1878, Dayton, Columbia, WA. Died, 30 June 1947, Dayton, Columbia, WA, age 69. They were both buried at the Dayton Cemetery.

248 ii. John Henry BEEMAN. Born, 8 Jan 1883, in Little Potlatch, Nez Perce, ID. Died, 10 May 1966, in Portland, Multnomah, OR, age 83. He married Margaret Evelyn "Maggie" BUCHANAN, daughter of Sy BUCHANAN and Martha Matilda CAMERON, 11 May 1913, in Joseph, Wallowa, OR. Born, 19 Aug 1888, New Westminister, B.C., Canada. Died 12 Apr 1971, Vancouver, Clark, WA, age 82. They were both buried at Enterprise, Wallowa, OR.

249 iii. Annie May BEEMAN. Born, 24 Nov 1885, in Little Potlatch, Nez Perce, ID. Died, 5 Apr 1935, in Enterprise, Wallowa, OR, age 49. She married James Ross WINTERS, son of Ross WINTERS, 7 Aug 1904, in Paradise, Wallowa, OR. Born, 20 Apr 1866, Boone, IA. Died, Nov 1937, Enterprise, Wallowa, OR, age 71. They were both buried at Paradise, OR.[86]

250 iv. Minnie Della BEEMAN. Born, 16 Sep 1886, in American Ridge, Nez Perce, ID. Died, 3 May 1972, in Walla Walla, WA, age 85. She married Clarence Oscar JOHNSON, son of James W. JOHNSON and Samantha PATTERSON, 4 Mar 1908, in Enterprise, Wallowa, OR. Born, 13 Feb 1881, Columbia, WA. Died 25 Nov 1957, Walla, Walla, WA, age 76. They were both buried at the Masonic Cemetery in Walla Walla, WA. He is listed in the 1913 Atlas as Proprietor, Summit View Farm near Turner, WA.[87]

251 v. Harry Richard BEEMAN. Born, 11 Feb 1889, in Little Potlatch, Nez Perce, ID. Died, 22 Apr 1890, in Little Potlatch, Nez Perce, ID, age 1.

252 vi. Charles Stirling BEEMAN. Born, 25 Apr 1891, in Moscow, Latah, ID. Died, 20 Apr 1964, in Enterprise, Wallowa, OR, age 73.

253 vii. Ralph Rufus BEEMAN. Born, 3 Feb 1894, in Lapwai Reservation, Nez Perce, ID. Died, 17 Dec 1980, in Portland, Multnomah, OR, age 86. Buried at Riverside, Okanogan, WA. He married Della Leota UTT, daughter of Earl Rudolph UTT and Jessie May GUANT, 10 Nov 1921, in Okanogan, Okanogan, WA. Born, 8 Jun 1901, Cedarvale, Chautauqua, KS. They were divorced in 1947.

254 viii. Grace Elizabeth BEEMAN. Born, 18 Feb 1896, in Imnaha, Wallowa, OR. Died, 27 Mar 1976, in Milton-Freewater, Umatilla, OR, age 80. She mar-

ried Newton Evin SASSER, son of Abraham H. SASSER and Margaret Elizabeth HAMMACK, 12 Jul 1912, in LaGrande, Union, OR. Born, 10 Feb 1891, London, Laurel, KY. Died, Jun 1985, Milton-Freewater, Umatilla, WA, age 94.

255 ix. Almedia Carolyn BEEMAN. Born, 7 May 1900, in Enterprise, Wallowa, OR. Died, 17 Feb 1990, in Kirkland, King, WA, age 89. She married Dorris Albert BOYER, son of Daniel Albert BOYER and Suzanna SIMMONS, 24 Apr 1920, in Vancouver, Clark, WA. Born, 13 Nov 1900, Richland, Baker, OR. Died, 11 Feb 1957, Portland, Multnomah, OR, age 56. They were both buried at the Rose City Cemetery, Portland, OR.

128. **Jefferson Davis "Dave"^{4} TURNER** (Charles Daniel, 39). Born, 8 Jan 1862, in Sedalia, Pettis, MO. Died, 13 Mar 1948, in Columbia, WA, age 86. He homesteaded near Turner, Columbia, WA.[88]

He married Margaret M. "Maggie" BALL, daughter of Isaac BALL and Margaret E. ROBBINS, 18 Jan 1885, in Washington, OR at the house of Isaac BALL. The witnesses were J. W. HAWES and T. L. TURNER. They were married by Geo. C. DAY, Justice of the Peace for Cedar Creek Precinct.[89] Born, 19 Dec 1865, in OR. Died, 26 Nov 1953, in Columbia, WA, age 87. Both were buried at the Dayton Cemetery.

They homesteaded in S25 T9 R38 in the section just south of his father on Ridge Road, 80 acres in 1885 and 160 acres in 1886. They also homesteaded near Turner, Columbia, WA where they farmed and raised a large family.[90] Children:[91]

+ 256 i. Charles Franklin^5 TURNER.
+ 257 ii. Myrtle Vivian TURNER.
258 iii. Samuel "Benjamin" TURNER. Born, 29 May 1889, in Columbia, WA. Died, 5 Mar 1972, in Columbia, WA, age 82. Buried at Dayton Cemetery.
+ 259 iv. Harry Hill TURNER.
260 v. Warren TURNER. Born, 1893, in Columbia, WA. Died, 1896, in Columbia, WA, age 3. Buried at Bundy Hollow Cemetery.
+ 261 vi. Anita Emma TURNER.
+ 262 vii. Zella Margaret TURNER.
263 viii. Forest O. "Bill" TURNER. Born, 4 Sep 1898, in

Columbia, WA. Died, May 1986, in Bend, Deschutes, OR, age 87. He married Alvina [UNKNOWN], 8 May 1939. Born, 18 Nov 1897. Died, Jul 1981, La Pine, Deschutes, OR, age 83.[92]

264 ix. Mary TURNER. Born, 12 Feb 1910, in Columbia, WA.

265 x. George Alton TURNER. Born, 5 Jul 1905, in Columbia, WA. Died, Sep 1955, in Columbia, WA, age 50.

\+ 266 xi. Daisy Fern TURNER.

267 xii. Darrel TURNER. Born, 1907, in Columbia, WA. Died, 1907, in Columbia, WA.

268 xiii. Lavetti Thomas "Buster" TURNER. Born, 7 Nov 1909, in Columbia, WA. He married Geraldine BELL, Jun 1939, in Coeur d'Alene, Kootenai, ID. Born, 1915, Spokane, WA. Died, Aug 1941, Salt Lake City, UT, age 26. He was living at 1011 S. 6th St., Dayton, WA in 1993.

129. **Mary Louisa**[4] TURNER (Charles Daniel, 39). Born, 24 Sep 1863, in Sedalia, Pettis, MO. Died, 25 Apr 1952, in Rosalia, Whitman, WA, age 88. They farmed near Plaza, Spokane, WA.

She married John William EVANS, son of William and Elizabeth M. EVANS, 21 Sep 1881, in Dayton, Columbia, WA. Born, 18 Mar 1857, in OR. Died, 5 Sep 1925, in Wenatchee, Chelan, WA, age 68. Both were buried at the Evergreen Cemetery in Rosalia, WA. He was the brother of Mary Louisa's step-mother, Marianna Eliza EVANS TURNER. William EVANS Sr. was a pioneer of Washington County, Oregon having arrived in 1852.[93] Children:[94]

269 i. Vincent "Clyde"[5] EVANS. Born, 20 Apr 1883, in Plaza, Spokane, WA. Died, 6 Sep 1959, in Rosalia, Whitman, WA, age 76. He married Florence KRUSE, 12 Apr 1915, in Portland, Multnomah, OR.

270 ii. Charles William EVANS. Born, 8 Jan 1885, in Plaza, Spokane, WA. Died, 3 Nov 1955, in Spokane, Spokane, WA, age 70. He married Maud Olive JAMES, 8 Jun 1904. Born, 22 Sep 1885, Knobnoster, Johnson, MO. Died, 27 Nov 1977, Spokane, Spokane, WA, age 92.[95]

271 iii. Stella M. EVANS. Born, 24 Sep 1887, in Plaza, Spokane, WA. Died, 19 Jun 1969, Spokane, Spo-

kane, WA, age 81. She married Luther SLINKARD, 18 Dec 1908. Died, 17 Nov 1969, Spokane, Spokane, WA. Both are buried at the Evergreen Cemetery in Rosalia, Whitman, WA.[96]

272 iv. Katie M. EVANS. Born, 14 Jan 1892, in Plaza, Spokane, WA. Died, 27 Feb 1970, Rosalia, Whitman, WA, age 78. She married John D. ROACH, 15 Apr 1914. Born, 8 Feb 1884. Died, 21 May 1972, Leavenworth, Chelan, WA, age 88.[97]

273 v. John William EVANS. Born, 12 Sep 1894, in Plaza, Spokane, WA. Died, 30 Dec 1973, Spokane, WA, age 79.[98] Resided, 1967, in Rosalia, Whitman, WA. He married Ruby SMITH, 14 Jul 1917.

274 vi. James T. EVANS. Born, 11 Nov 1896, in Plaza, Spokane, WA. He married Ruth MUELLER, 21 Feb 1921. Born, 21 Sep 1898. Died, 27 Nov 1988, Cashmere, Chelan, WA, age 90.[99]

275 vii. Wilson L. EVANS. Born, 28 Jun 1899, in Plaza, Spokane, WA. Died, 31 Mar 1980, Wenatchee, Chelan, WA, age 81.[100] He married Esther SMOUSE, 21 Feb 1921. Born, 22 Oct 1900. Died, Sep 1981, Peshastin, Chelan, WA, age 80.[101]

276 viii. Henry L. EVANS. Born, 3 Jul 1902, in Plaza, Spokane, WA. Died, 5 Aug 1932, age 30. He married Grace CHILDRESS, 1923.

131. **Lilly Lenora^4 TURNER** (Charles Daniel, 39). Born, 3 Jul 1873, in Oregon City, Clackamas, OR. Died, 27 Dec 1950, age 77. Her father, Charles TURNER, was living with them in the 1900, Star Precinct, Columbia, WA census.

She married John H. BIGGART, 15 Nov 1893, in Dayton, Columbia, WA, at the Methodist Episcopal Parsonage.[102] Born, 1 Jun 1862, in IA. Died, 9 Oct 1933, Mohler, Lewis, ID, age 71. They were both buried at the Nez Perce Cemetery.

John BIGGART moved to the Pacific coast in 1888 and later settled at Dayton. He moved to Mohler in 1903.[103] John B. DAVIS built the first hotel in Mohler, Lewis, ID. It was taken over by John BIGGART [about 1905], who also ran a livery barn, which he continued long after he no longer operated the hotel.[104] After the railroad was built to Vollmer, John BIGGART drove to Vollmer, got the mail from the train, and delivered it to the Fletcher and Mohler Post Offices.[105] John H. BIGGART and family were on the 1910 census at Mohler where he was listed as a Liveryman. In the 1920 census they were at Nez Perce City, Lewis, ID. Children:[106]

277 i. Glen A.^{5} BIGGART. Born, 28 Nov 1894, in Columbia, WA. Died, 18 Feb 1959, in Lincoln, WA, age 64.[107] He married Madge MILLER, daughter of Perry MILLER, 10 Jul 1922. Born, 13 Nov 1896, at Nezperce, Lewis, ID. Died, 7 Jun 1976, at Spokane, WA, age 79. Lived in Harrington, Lincoln, WA from 1923 until his death in 1959.[108]

278 ii. Marie BIGGART. Born, Feb 1896, in Columbia, WA. She married William HARBKE of Hardest, Alberta, Canada. Lived in Seattle. Died (before 1986) possibly with daughter Wilhemina who lives at Lewiston, ID.

279 iii. Bula BIGGART. Born, 10 Jan 1899, in Columbia, WA. Died, Apr 1986, in Nezperce, Lewis, ID, age 87. She married William DOGGETT, 21 Dec 1919, at Nezperce. Born, 26 Jan 1898. Died, 1 Apr 1946, age 48. Both were buried at the Nezperce Cemetery.[109]

280 iv. John Leo BIGGART. Born, 17 Jun 1904, in Mohler, Nez Perce, ID. Died, 29 Dec 1910, in Nezperce of Spinal Meningitis, age 6. Buried by his parents in the Nezperce Cemetery.[110]

281 v. Raymond BIGGART. Born, 1911, in Lewis, ID. Died before 1986. Living in Mohler in 1933.

282 vi. Vera BIGGART. Born, 1914, in Lewis, ID. Died in Seattle, King, WA after 1986. Married, Ray BRANOM. (Son, Bob BRANOM of KIRO News in Seattle, born 11 Jun 1942.)

132. **Edward Daniel^4 TURNER** (Charles Daniel, 39). Born, 4 Sep 1876, in Columbia, WA. Died of coronary thrombosis, 29 Aug 1940, Lewiston, Nez Perce, ID, age 62.

He married Orlena ROBERTS, daughter of Andrew M. and Mary Jane ROBERTS, 25 Nov 1895, in Asotin, WA. Born, 13 Feb 1876, in Clay, KY. Died, 5 Jan 1966, Clarkston, Asotin, WA, age 89. They are both buried at the Independent Order of Odd Fellows Cemetery at Craigmont, ID. The cemetery inscriptions are, Edward David TURNER, 1875-1946, husband of Orlena; Orlena R. TURNER, 1876-1966, wife of Edward D.[111]

They were in Nez Perce Precinct in Nez Perce County, ID on the 1900 census. In the 1910 census they were at Kamiah, Nez Perce County which was then formed into Lewis County in 1911. They lived on Camas Prairie, at Mohler, Lewis, ID. In fact, a tree and a pumphouse from their place are the only landmarks left on the townsite of Mohler.[112] Children:

+ 283 i. Marvin D.[5] TURNER.
+ 284 ii. Melvin Verner TURNER.
+ 285 iii. Otis Elgin TURNER.

133. **Vivian Winfred[4] TURNER** (Charles Daniel, 39). Born, Jun 1878, in Dayton, Columbia, WA. Died, 20 May 1924, age 45.

He married Cora B. CROSSLER, daughter of J. A. and Nancy CROSSLER,[113] 8 Oct 1896, in Dayton, Columbia, WA. Born, 22 Feb 1879, in WA. Died, Jun 1964, age 85. Both were buried in the Dayton Cemetery. They were on the 1900 Bundy precinct, Columbia, WA census. They moved to Lewiston in 1911 and ran the University Grocery for many years. On the 1920 Lewiston, Nez Perce, ID census they are living at 1524 - 3rd St. Child:

286 i. Homer[5] TURNER. Born, 11 Apr 1898, in Columbia, WA. Died, 5 Jan 1981, in Lewiston, Nez Perce, ID, age 82. Buried at the Dayton Cemetery. He attended the University of Washington and served in the Navy in 1918. He began his Nez Perce County employment in Oct 1920 in the treasurer's office, moving to the auditor's office in 1940 where he was deputy auditor, retiring in 1966. Before moving to the Orchards Nursing Home he lived at the same address on 3rd Street where the family had lived since 1920.[114]

135. **Mary Frances[4] TURNER** (Thomas Lee, 40). Born, 31 Mar 1862, in MO. Died, 11 Sep 1944, in Marion, OR, age 82.[115]

She married Frederick A. ELLIGSEN, 6 Jan 1881, in Clackamas, OR.[116] Born, May 1852, in Canada. Died, 17 Jan 1931, in Clackamas, OR, age 78.[117] Both were buried at the Bird Cemetery, Stafford, OR. They were on the 1900 and 1920 East Cedar Precinct, Washington, OR census. Children:

287 i. Henry E.[5] ELLIGSEN. Born, 14 Nov 1881, in

Clackamas, OR. Died, 7 Feb 1911, in Clackamas, OR, age 29. Buried at the Bird Cemetery.

288 ii. Anna M. ELLIGSEN. Born, 11 Oct 1883, in Clackamas, OR. Died, 15 May 1890, in Clackamas, OR, age 6. Buried at the Bird Cemetery.

289 iii. Helena C. ELLIGSEN. Born, Aug 1887, in Clackamas, OR. She married [Unknown] SEELY.

290 iv. Ella R. M. ELLIGSEN. Born, Dec 1891, in Clackamas, OR. She married [Unknown] PETERS.

291 v. Rosa M. ELLIGSEN. Born, Feb 1893, in Clackamas, OR. She married [Unknown] BURKERT.

292 vi. Albert F. ELLIGSEN. Born, Apr 1895, in Clackamas, OR.

136. **Julia Elizabeth^4 TURNER** (Thomas Lee, 40). Born, 24 Nov 1863, in MO. Died, 2 Feb 1935, Marion, OR, age 71.[118]

She married Edwin Ruthborn SEELY, 25 Jun 1883, in Clackamas, OR.[119] Born, May 1862, in OR. Died, 28 May 1924, Marion, OR, age 62.[120] They were on the 1900 and 1910 census in Monitor Precinct, Marion, OR. Children:

293 i. Harry B.^{5} SEELY. Born, Jul 1884, in Marion, OR.

294 ii. Perry W. SEELY. Born, Sep 1886, in Marion, OR. He married Nelly E. KUNTZ, 1908, in Marion, OR. Born, KS.[121]

295 iii. Lucius "Roy" SEELY. Born, Nov 1888, in Marion, OR.

296 iv. Thomas "Lee" SEELY. Born, 27 Jan 1891, in Marion, OR, Died, 22 Dec 1987, age 96. He married Elsie Mary [UNKNOWN], 29 Nov 1911, in Woodburn, Clackamas, OR. From a newspaper article of unknown origin: "Lee SEELY, fourth boy of a family of seven boys and five girls, was born on his parents' 103 acres farm in Woodburn. He has four sisters living; two in Oregon, and two in California."[122]

297 v. Ruth Elizabeth SEELY. Born, Jun 1893, in Marion, OR, d. 26 Aug 1989 in CA, age 96. She married [Unknown] AKER.

298 vi. Percy H. SEELY. Born, Jul 1897, in Marion, OR.

299 vii. Julia Edna SEELY. Born, Jan 1900, in Marion, OR. She married [Unknown] STINGER.

300 viii. Ethel SEELY. Born, 1902, in Marion, OR.

301 ix. Dennis SEELY. Born, 1905, in Marion, OR.

302 x. Edith SEELY. Born, 1907, in Marion, OR. She married [Unknown] LUCHT.

137. **John Marion⁴ TURNER** (Thomas Lee, 40). Born, 30 Apr 1865, on the wagon train trip to Oregon. Died, 11 Feb 1938, Clackamas, OR, age 72.[123]

He married Jessie M. DAY, daughter of George C. DAY and Sarah Jane PAINTER, 7 Dec 1884, Washington, OR at the house of Geo. C. DAY. Witnesses were J. H. DAY and David TURNER. Geo. C. DAY, Justice of the Peace for Cedar Precinct.[124] Born, 1868, in OR. Her father was a pioneer of Washington County, Oregon having arrived in 1852. At one time he purchased an interest in the old Hosier steamboat that sailed between Oregon City and Dayton. He owned 320 acres 2½ miles south of Tualatin and had 15 children. In a history written in 1893 he reported that his daughter, Jessie, resided in Walla Walla.[125] Children:

303 i. Sarah Elizabeth[5] TURNER. Born, 1886, in Walla Walla, WA.[126]

304 ii. George V. TURNER. Born, 1888, in OR. He married May M. BROOKS HARTMAN, 13 Jun 1911, in Yakima, WA. Born, 1885, in KS. They were on the 1920 census living on Tacoma Ave. in Sunnyside, Yakima, WA with no children. On this census he was reported as born in Oregon.

She married 2nd, Schuyler J. ADAMS, 13 Oct 1895, in Walla Walla, WA, by Lee A. JOHNSON, Minister. Witnesses: George DAY and Robert J. DAY [her brothers].

He married 2nd, Lena M. BOWER, 1898. Born, 1870, in IL. Died, 4 Jan 1950, in Multnomah, OR, age 79.[127] Her parents were born in Germany. John and Lena were living with Benjamin M. TURNER(118) on the 1900 census in Covello, Columbia, WA. On the 1910 census of Tualatin, Clackamas, OR they were reported as married for 12 years. It was the second marriage for both. Lena had two children by her first marriage. In 1920 they were living at 15th and Walnut streets in West Linn, Clackamas, OR.

139. **James Arthur[4] TURNER** (Thomas Lee, 40). Born, 27 May 1870, in Clackamas, OR. Died, 22 Sep 1959, in Walla Walla, WA, age 89. He was buried at the Dayton Cemetery. He was living in Malheur, OR in the 1920 census, while his children were living to-

gether in Dayton, Columbia, WA. He was living in Condon, Gilliam, OR in the year of the death of his daughter Hattie Mae [1931].

He married, Wilhelmina "Minnie" PRIESTER, 8 Mar 1893, in Clackamas, OR.[128] Born, 29 Oct 1868,[129] in IA. Died, 28 Jul 1915, in OR, age 46.[130] Buried at the Turner Cemetery, Columbia, WA. They moved to Turner, Columbia, WA in 1904. Children:[131]

+ 305 i. Arthur Smith[5] TURNER.
+ 306 ii. Lloyd Julius TURNER.
+ 307 iii. Lillie Nancy Otillia TURNER.
308 iv. Goldie Agnes TURNER. Born, 1 Apr 1902, in Clackamas, OR. Died, 13 Dec 1983, in Dayton, Columbia, WA, age 81. Buried at the Dayton Cemetery. She worked at Central Cleaners in Walla Walla until 1947, when she and her brother established the Odessa Cleaners in Odessa, WA. In 1963 they purchased the Dayton Cleaners.[132]
+ 309 v. Gladys Ellen TURNER.
+ 310 vi. Hattie Mae TURNER.
+ 311 vii. Thomas Jeffries TURNER.

140. **Albert F.[4] TURNER** (Thomas Lee, 40). Born, 25 Jan 1872, in Clackamas, OR. Died, 11 Feb 1912, in Clackamas, OR, age 39.[133] Buried at the Bird Cemetery.

He married, Kate E. MILEY, 20 Oct 1897.[134] Born, circa 1874, in OR. Died, 6 Apr 1951, Marion, OR.[135] In the 1910 census of Tualatin, Clackamas, OR, they were reported as having been married 12 years and had two children. Children:

312 i. Forest C. TURNER. Born, 1905, Clackamas, OR.
313 ii. Florence TURNER. Born, 1906, Clackamas, OR.

She married 2nd, George T. ANGEL. They were on the 1920 census at Wilsonville, Clackamas, OR with the two TURNER children.

141. **Ella Harriet[4] TURNER** (Thomas Lee, 40). Born, 1 Sep 1874, in Clackamas, OR. Died, 30 Oct 1951, Clackamas, OR, age 77.[136]

She married John SEEDLING, 22 Nov 1894, Clackamas, OR. Born, Oct 1864, in Canada. Died, 15 Oct 1944, Clackamas, OR, age 80.[137] They are on the 1900 and 1920 Tualatin, Clackamas, OR census. Children:

314 i. Sidney SEEDLING. Born, 17 Oct 1898, Clackamas, OR. Died, Jan 1971, Oregon City, Clackamas, OR, age 72.[138]

315 ii. Eva SEEDLING. Born, May 1900, Clackamas, OR. She married [Unknown] CHAPMAN.

142. **Herbert T.⁴ TURNER** (Thomas Lee, 40). Born, 16 Jun 1876, in Clackamas, OR. Died, 26 Feb 1912, in Clackamas, OR, age 35.[139] Buried at the Bird Cemetery. He was on the 1900 Covello, Columbia, WA census working for Ben TURNER(118).

He married Elizabeth "Lizzie" M. SCHISMER[?], 1902. Born, c1885, in Germany. In the 1910 census of Tualatin, Clackamas, OR, they were reported as having been married 8 years and had four children, three of whom were living. Children:

316 i. Mabel TURNER. Born, 1903, Clackamas, OR.

317 ii. Thomas D. TURNER. Born, 27 Feb 1905, Clackamas, OR. Died, May 1985, Milwaukie, Clackamas, OR, age 80.[140]

318 iii. Elsie TURNER. Born, 1907, Clackamas, OR.

143. **Lilley "Susie"⁴ TURNER** (Thomas Lee, 40). Born, 4 Nov 1880, in Clackamas, OR. Died, 23 Feb 1955.

She married Michael GROSS, 9 Jun 1898, Clackamas, OR. Born, Jan 1873, in Russia. Died, 28 Oct 1937, Clackamas, OR, age 64.[141] They are on the 1900 Tualatin and 1920 Oregon City, Clackamas, OR census living at 223 Main St. Child:

319 i. Hattie C. GROSS. Born, Jan 1900, Clackamas, OR. She married [Unknown] SCHEER.

144. **Charles E.⁴ TURNER** (Thomas Lee, 40). Born, 9 Nov 1882, in Clackamas, OR. Died, 27 Oct 1969, in Dayton, Columbia, WA, age 86.[142]

He married Nettie Luella AKER, 21 Oct 1908, in Woodburn, Marion, OR, by Judge HAYES. Born, 24 Aug 1883, in Kellerton, Ringgold, IA. Died, 3 Mar 1963, in Dayton, Columbia, WA, age 79. Both were buried in the Dayton Cemetery.

After spending the early years of their married life farming near Wilsonville, OR, they moved to Columbia County in May, 1911. They were on the 1910 Tualatin, Clackamas, OR census and the 1920, Turner, Columbia, WA census. They farmed the old HOWARD place in the Turner district and also farmed in the Whetstone district. They retired and moved to Dayton in 1951 where Mr. TURNER had the hobby of raising roses and flowers. He had 65 different rose varieties around his home on South Fourth Street. He was a member of the Cattlemen's Association and the Columbia County Farm Bureau. Mrs. TURNER was a member of the Columbia County Cow Belles and the Covello Thimble Bee. Child:[143]

320 i. Lloyd Benton⁵ TURNER. Born, 13 Sep 1910, in Clackamas, OR. Died, 11 Jul 1931, in Dayton, Columbia, WA, age 20. Buried in the Dayton Cemetery.

145. **Smith^4 TURNER** (Thomas Lee, 40). Born, 21 Sep 1883, in Clackamas, OR. Died, 28 Oct 1945, in Clackamas, OR, age 62.[144]

He married Ida May BOWERS, 21 Dec 1904, in Clackamas, OR. Born, 1886, in OR. Died, 18 Jan 1940, in Clackamas, OR, age 53.[145] Both were buried at the Bird Cemetery in Stafford. They were on the 1910 and 1920 census in Tualatin precinct. Children:

321 i. Nola P.^{5} TURNER. Born, 1905, in Clackamas, OR. She married [Unknown] MURALT.

322 ii. Norman A. TURNER. Born, 15 Sep 1906, in Clackamas, OR. Died, Apr 1974, in West Linn, Clackamas, OR, age 67.[146]

323 iii. Howard S. TURNER. Born, 10 Jun 1908, in Clackamas, OR. Died, Jan 1982, in Oregon City, Clackamas, OR, age 73.[147]

324 iv. Beryl M. TURNER. Born, 1917, in Clackamas, OR. She married [Unknown] HOLMAN.

NOTES: CHAPTER 4 - FOURTH GENERATION

---

[1] D. W. Meinig, *The Great Columbia Plain: A Historical Geography, 1805-1910* (Seattle: University of Washington Press, 1968), pp. 294-298.

[2] Arnold & Esther Pearson, *Early Churches of Washington State* (Seattle: University of Washington Press, 1980), p. 136; *An Illustrated History of Southeastern Washington including Walla Walla, Columbia, Garfield and Asotin Counties, Washington* (Spokane: Western Historical Publishing Co., 1906), p. 166.

[3] Ellis and Elvira Ellen Laidlaw, *Wait's Mill: The Story of the Community of Waitsburg, Washington* (Chicago: Adams Press, 1970), p. 115.

[4] Meinig, *Great Columbia Plain*, p. 236.

[5] Fletcher, *Early Columbia County*, p. 103.

[6] *Ibid.*, pp. 233-234.

[7] *Ibid.*, p. 223; *Illustrated History of Southeastern Washington*, p. 302.

[8] Meining, *Great Columbia Plain*, pp. 248-249; *Illustrated History of Southeastern Washington*, p. 303.

[9] Meining, *Great Columbia Plain*, pp. 242, 257-258; Rinehart, *Covello*, pp. 98-99; Fletcher, *Early Columbia County*, p. 90.

[10] *Biographical History of Crawford, Ida and Sac Counties, Iowa*, pp. 396-397.

[11] Ewing, *My Turner Family*, p. 3.

[12] Ewing, *My Turner Family*, p. 5.

[13] Pilot Rock, Oregon newspaper.

[14] Oregon Death Index 1931-1941, Film #1,373,873.

[15] Oregon Death Index 1921-1931, Film #1,373,872.

[16] Oregon Death Index 1903-1921, Film #1,373,870.

[17] Gilbert, *Historic Sketches*, p. 65 of appendix.

[18] Social Security File; Washington State Death Index.

[19] Social Security File; Oregon Death Index 1961-1971, Film #1,373,876 where his wife's name is Dora.

[20] Washington State Death Index.

[21] Washington State Death Index.

[22] Greenwood Park Grange, *Pioneers of the Columbia* (Colville, WA: 1965), pp. 22, 69-70.

[23] *Columbia County Chronicle*, 18 Nov 1916.

[24] *Columbia County News*, December 1928.

[25] Greenwood Park Grange, *Pioneers of the Columbia*, pp. 69-70.

[26] *Ibid.*, p. 67.

[27] Washington State Death Index.

[28] Washington State Death Index.
[29] Washington State Death Index.
[30] Washington State Death Index.
[31] *Columbia County News*, 24 Aug 1907.
[32] Social Security File.
[33] Washington State Death Index.
[34] Social Security File.
[35] Social Security File.
[36] Washington State Death Index.
[37] Washington State Death Index.
[38] Social Security File and Washington State Death Index.
[39] Information supplied on this family by Helen HENRY in 1968.
[40] Rinehart, *Covello*, p. 246.
[41] Social Security File.
[42] Rinehart, *Covello*, pp. 81-82.
[43] Social Security File.
[44] Social Security File.
[45] *Lyman's History of Old Walla Walla*, pp. 721-722.
[46] George A. Ogle, *Standard Atlas of Columbia County, Washington* (Chicago: 1913), Patron's Reference Directory.
[47] Rinehart, *Covello*, picture pages between pp. 73-74.
[48] Rinehart, *Covello*, pp. 89-90.
[49] Washington State Death Index.
[50] Washington State Death Index.
[51] George A. Ogle, *Standard Atlas of Walla Walla County, Washington* (Chicago: 1909), map.
[52] *Columbia County News*, 12 Jan 1907.
[53] Ogle, *Standard Atlas of Walla Walla County*, Patron's Reference Directory.
[54] *Columbia County News*, 7 Dec 1907.
[55] Ogle, *Standard Atlas of Columbia County*, Patron's Reference Directory.
[56] *Columbia County News*, 4 May 1889, 28 Aug 1889.
[57] Washington State Death Index.
[58] Washington State Death Index.
[59] Lyman, *Old Walla Walla County*, pp. 148-149; see also Rinehart, *Covello*, pp. 59-61.
[60] Washington State Death Index.
[61] Washington State Death Index.
[62] Washington State Death Index.
[63] Washington State Death Index.
[64] Washington State Death Index.
[65] Social Security File.
[66] Social Security File.
[67] Rinehart, *Covello*, p. 61.

[68] Washington State Death Index.
[69] Rinehart, *Covello*, p. 71.
[70] Letters from Irene BARGER in 1968.
[71] *Columbia Chronicle*, 4 March 1922.
[72] *Frontier Justice*, Walla Walla Civil Court, Case #2087.
[73] Rinehart, *Covello*, pp. 51, 71.
[74] *Columbia County News*, 5 Dec 1908.
[75] *Columbia County News*, 6 Mar 1909.
[76] *Washington Pioneers*, I:155, submitted by Norma BROOKS, Rt. 3, Box 372, Longview, TX 75603.
[77] His name was James E. on the 1889 and 1900 census, but named as Joseph Edgar by his descendant, Norma BROOKS, who submitted the information on the family in *Washington Pioneers*, I:155.
[78] Washington State Death Index.
[79] Washington State Death Index.
[80] Social Security File.
[81] Washington State Death Index.
[82] Northeast Washington Genealogical Society, *Presents Our Washington State Centennial Project, Enumeration of Stevens County Cemeteries: Book Three, Rural Area Cemeteries*, (Colville, WA: 1989), p. 60; Mildred Dashiell Ellsworth, *Who Was Who in the Cedonia Cemetery* (included in the above book), p. 74.
[83] Greenwood Park Grange, *Pioneers of the Columbia*, pp. 15, 103.
[84] Ellsworth, *Who Was Who in the Cedonia Cemetery*, p. 60. There must be a typing error in the date.
[85] For a complete history of this family see, Gwen BOYER BJORKMAN, *The Descendants of Thomas Beeman of Kent, Connecticut* (Bellevue, WA: 1971), pp. 96-97, 114-120.
[86] *The History of Wallowa County, Oregon* (Enterprise: Wallowa County Museum Board, 1983), p. 380.
[87] Ogle, *Standard Atlas of Columbia County*, Patron's Reference Directory.
[88] Rinehart, *Covello*, p. 71.
[89] Washington County, Oregon Marriages, 3:145.
[90] Rinehart, *Covello*, p. 71.
[91] Information on this family supplied by Dixie VERSTOPPEN, 2806 SW Marshall, Pendleton, OR, in 1969 and Harry Hill TURNER, 416 E. Clay, Dayton, WA, in 1968.
[92] Social Security File.
[93] Oregon Donation Land Claim.
[94] Information on this family supplied by Ruby EVANS, Rt. 2, Box 31, Rosalia, WA, in 1967.
[95] Information on this family supplied by Cathie MAGNUSON, 52178 SE 4th, Scappoose, OR 97056, in 1993.

[96] Washington State Death Index; Obituaries in the *Spokane Spokesman Review*, 21 Jun 1969, 19 Nov 1969.
[97] Washington State Death Index; Social Security File.
[98] Washington State Death Index; Social Security File.
[99] Social Security File.
[100] Washington State Death Index.
[101] Social Security File.
[102] *Columbia County News*, 18 Nov 1893.
[103] Obituary from the *Nezperce Herald*, 12 Oct 1933 and the Nezperce Cemetery records.
[104] Jo Thomason, ***Highlands of Craig Mountain*** (Highland Press: 1984), pp. 200-201.
[105] Margaret Nell Longeteig, ***Remember When***, (Lapwai, ID: Nez Perce Printing, 1976), p. 73.
[106] Information on this family supplied by Margaret Nell LONGETEIG, 415 Stewart Ave., Lewiston, ID 83501, in 1993.
[107] *Columbia County News*, 1 Dec 1894; Social Security File.
[108] Obituary from the *Lewiston Morning Tribune*, Jun 1976 and the *Nezperce Herald*, 17 Jun 1976.
[109] Obituary from the *Lewiston Morning Tribune*, 16 Apr 1986.
[110] Nezperce Cemetery records.
[111] Letter from Homer TURNER(289), PO Box 105, Lewiston, ID, 10 Oct 1967.
[112] Death Certificate, Funeral Record, Letter from Jo THOMASON, Box 96, Craigmont, ID 83523; Thomason, *Craig Mountain*, p. 201; Letter from Margaret Nell LONGETEIG, 23 June 1993.
[113] 1880 Dayton, Columbia County, Washington Census, p. 109.
[114] Social Security File, obituary in *Lewiston Morning Tribune*, 6 Jan 1981.
[115] Oregon Death Index 1941-1951, Film #1,373,874.
[116] Clackamas County, Oregon Marriages, 3:75.
[117] Oregon Death Index 1931-1941, Film #1,373,873.
[118] Oregon Death Index 1931-1941, Film #1,373,873.
[119] Clackamas County, Oregon Marriages, 3:163.
[120] Oregon Death Index 1921-1931, Film #1,373,872.
[121] 1910 Monitor Precinct, Marion County, Oregon Census, p. 217.
[122] Information on this family supplied by Virgil E. AKER, 44927 Laszlo St., Lancaster, CA 93534, in 1993.
[123] Oregon Death Index 1931-1941, Film #1,373,873.
[124] Washington County, Oregon Marriages, 3:140.
[125] Harvey Kimball Hines, ***An Illustrated History of the State of Oregon*** (Chicago: Lewis Pub. Co., 1893), p. 1241.
[126] 1887 Walla Walla, Washington Territorial Census, p. 148.
[127] Oregon Death Index 1941-1951, Film #1,373,874.
[128] Clackamas County, Oregon Marriages, 5:159.
[129] Kae FLETCHER reports that she was born 19 Oct 1874.

130 Oregon Death Index 1903-1921, Film #1,373,870.
131 Rinehart, *Covello*, p. 70.
132 Washington State Death Index; Obituary from Kae FLETCHER.
133 Clackamas County, Oregon Death Records, 1:62; Oregon Death Index 1903-1921, Film #1,373,870 has date of death as 17 Feb 1912.
134 Clackamas County, Oregon Marriage Records, 6:457.
135 Oregon Death Index 1951-1961, Film #1,373,875.
136 Oregon Death Index 1951-1961, Film #1,373,875.
137 Oregon Death Index 1941-1951, Film #1,373,874.
138 Social Security File.
139 Clackamas County, Oregon Death Records, 1:62; Oregon Death Index 1903-1921, Film #1,373,870
140 Social Security File.
141 Oregon Death Index 1931-1941, Film #1,373,873.
142 Washington State Death Index.
143 Rinehart, *Covello*, p. 71; letter from C. E. TURNER(144), Dayton, WA, dated 12 Feb 1968; newspaper article about their Golden Wedding Reception (1958) sent by Kae FLETCHER.
144 Oregon Death Index 1941-1951, Film #1,373,874.
145 Oregon Death Index 1931-1941, Film #1,373,873.
146 Social Security File.
147 Social Security File.

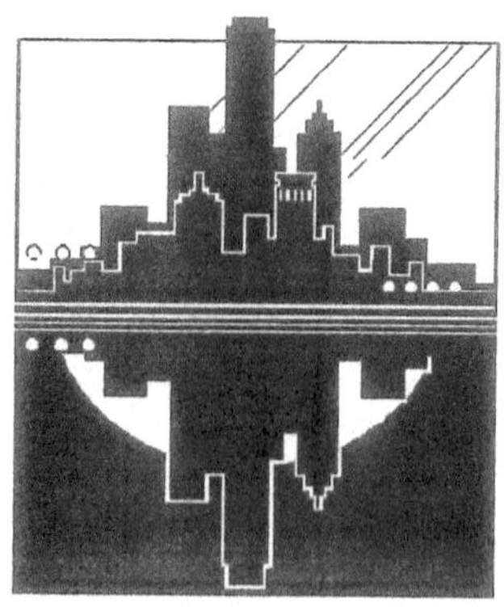

CHAPTER 5

THE FIFTH GENERATION

The fifth generation of the children of John Meridy TURNER(1) lived in Missouri, Iowa, Illinois, Indiana, Kansas, California, Idaho, Oregon and Washington. Some stayed on the farm, but many more moved to the city. With the advent of the automobile, it became even easier for the farmers to go to the city for shopping and recreation and the small farm towns died.

Two wars and two depressions helped put an end to the family farm. In Columbia County, wheat sold for $2.50 a bushel in 1920 and .87¢ a bushel in 1921. By 1928 it was at an all time low of .25¢ a bushel. Many young men entered the service during wartime and never returned to the family farm.

There are few places better suited to big scale farming than Columbia County. By leaving one half the acreage idle or fallow (summerfallow) each year, the yield increases but this means the acreage requirements are double of elsewhere. The expense of present day equipment is another reason for large scale farming.

Custom farming had become a trend. The farmer-owner runs the farm, but hires the work custom done. In 1975 James and Lawrence TURNER and their sons Randy and Richard were custom farming 2,572 acres which included the Edna GWINN, Claude POLLY and Fred MCCAULEY farms.[1]

It is good to take a look back into the past and remember where we came from. In successive generations our family moved from Virginia, to Ohio, to Missouri, to Oregon and then to Washington. Family life has changed in this country since the time when we all lived on farms, but our family values should stay the same. The home, the church and the school are the institutions that form us and form our country.

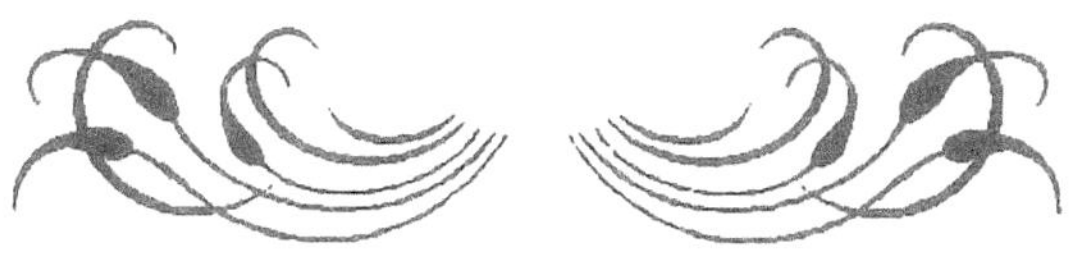

FIFTH GENERATION

154. **Viola**^{5} **TURNER** (James T., 46). Born, Jul 1862, in Clark, MO. They were in Catlin, Marion, KS in the 1900 and 1920 census.

She married Green STOVALL, 6 Sep 1878, in Crawford, IA. Born, Mar 1858, in MO. Children:

325 i. Charles^6 STOVALL. Born, Sep 1879, in Crawford, IA.
326 ii. Roy STOVALL. Born, Jun 1883, in Marion, KS.
327 iii. Blanche STOVALL. Born, Aug 1887, in Marion, KS.
328 iv. Mattie STOVALL. Born, Mar 1893, in Marion, KS.

155. **Edwin**^{5} **TURNER** (James T., 46). Born, Mar 1865, in IL. They were in the 1900 Milford, Crawford, IA census.

He married Cora [UNKNOWN], 1892. Born, Apr 1878, in IN. Children:

329 i. Lettie^6 TURNER. Born, May 1893, in KS.
330 ii. Leslie TURNER. Born, Apr 1895, in IL.
331 iii. Howard TURNER. Born, May 1897, in IA.
332 iv. Katie TURNER. Born, Jul 1899, in KS.

163. **Milliard J.**^{5} **TURNER** (James T., 46). Born, Nov 1882, in Crawford, IA. They were in the 1920 Denison, Crawford, IA census living at 328 Railroad Ave.

He married Alice [UNKNOWN], 1905, in IA. Born, 1886, in IA. Children:

333 i. Ione K.^{6} TURNER. Born, 1906, in Crawford, IA.
334 ii. Bruce M. TURNER. Born, 1912, in Crawford, IA.
335 iii. Harold R. TURNER. Born, 1915, in Crawford, IA.

169. **William H.**^{5} **TURNER** (John Alexander, 49). Born, Sep 1868, in Clark, MO. Died, 1944, in Scotland, MO, age 76.

He married Nannie C. JAMES, 15 Dec 1893, in MO. Born, May 1872, in VA. Died, 1948, in Scotland, MO, age 76. They were both buried at the Wyaconda Cemetery. They were in the 1900 census Washington, Clark, MO where he was a farmer and on the 1920 Wyaconda, Clark, MO census living on Main Street. Children:

336 i. W. Hubert^{6} TURNER. Born, circa 1895, in Scotland, MO. Died in Memphis, Scotland, MO. He married Vera GRISTY, 13 Oct 1923, in Scotland, MO. Resided in Memphis, MO where she was Clerk to the Probate Judge.[2]

\+ 337 ii. Hazel G. TURNER.

338 iii. John Milton TURNER. Born, 1914, in MO. Resided in Obion, TN in 1968.

170. **Florence G."Jennie"**^{5} **TURNER** (John Alexander, 49). Born, Apr 1872, in Clark, MO.

She married Edgar L. SUTER of Fairmont, Clark, MO, 9 Sep 1891, in Scotland, MO. Born, Nov 1865, in MO. They are on the 1900 Harrison, Scotland, MO census.

339 i. Earl^{6} SUTER. Born, Nov 1892, in MO.

172. **Thadius**^{5} **TURNER** (John Alexander, 49). Born, Jun 1877, in Clark, MO. Died, Feb 1945, in Clark, MO, age 67.

He married Lena BLATTNER in MO. Born, Jan 1880, in MO. Died, 1954, age 74. They were on the 1900 Washington, Clark, MO and the 1920 Wyaconda, Clark, census. Children:

340 i. Berneice^{6} TURNER. Born, Jan 1900, in Clark, MO. She married Lyman BISHOP.

341 ii. Clarice TURNER. Born, circa 1903, in Clark, MO. She married [Unknown] LANE.

173. **Nellie E.**^{5} **TURNER** (John Alexander, 49). Born, 1879, in Clark, MO. She was still living in 1968 in MO.[3]

She married, first, Ben BERTRAM. Child:

342 i. Velma E.[6] BERTRAM. Born, 1902, Clark, MO. She married George BORDERS.

She married, second, Wilbur J. RITCHIE. Born, 1880. Died, before 1968. They were living on Walnut Street on the 1920 Wyaconda, Clark, MO census.

175. **Lottie Gertrude**[5] **TURNER** (John Alexander, 49). Born, May 1890, in Clark, MO. Living in Wyaconda, Clark, MO in 1968.

She married Virgil B. LAFRENZ, 23 Feb 1921, in Clark, MO. Child:

343 i. Helen Marjorie[6] LAFRENZ. Born, 27 Jun 1928, in MO. She married Oliver ELAM, 26 May 1946.

182. **Frankie**[5] **TURNER** (Andrew Jackson, 57). Born, circa 1875, in Scotland, MO.

She married Ed WILSON. Child:

344 i. Rita[6] WILSON. She married George W. VARNADO.

232. **Grover Thomas**[5] **TURNER** (John Thomas, 121). Born, 4 Dec 1884, in Columbia, WA. Died, 16 Sep 1949, in Dayton, Columbia, WA, age 64. Buried at the Dayton Cemetery.

He married Beatrice Emma LACROIX, 1915. Born, 26 Jul 1900. Children:[4]

345 i. Leonard John[6] TURNER. Born, 10 Apr 1917, in Hythe, Alberta, Can. Died, 9 Dec 1951, in Dayton, Columbia, WA, age 34. Buried at Dayton Cemetery.
\+ 346 ii. Vivian Irene TURNER.
\+ 347 iii. Laura Jean TURNER.
\+ 348 iv. Grover Robert TURNER.
\+ 349 v. Ben Delbert TURNER.
350 vi. Darlene Fay TURNER. Born, 23 Sep 1932, in

Dayton, Columbia, WA. Died, 29 Aug 1950, in Dayton, Columbia, WA, age 17.

+ 351 vii. Thomas Lee TURNER.

234. **Cora "Irene"[5] TURNER** (John Thomas, 121). Born, 30 Sep 1888, in Columbia, WA. Died, 20 Mar 1975, in Walla Walla, WA, age 86.

She married Delbert A. BARGER, 1911. Born, 23 Aug 1889. Died, 13 Mar 1973, in Walla Walla, WA, age 83. Child:[5]

352 i. Agnes Louise[6] BARGER. She married Ken MAXON.

235. **Clarence Roy[5] TURNER** (John Thomas, 121). Born, 4 Jan 1891, in Columbia, WA. Died, 10 Jan 1963, in George, Grant, WA, age 72. Buried at Quincy, Grant, WA.

He married Iva HUGHES, 23 Dec 1915, in Princeton, BC, Can. Born, 19 Jun 1898, in Monticello, White, IN. Children:[6]

353 i. Altha Lois[6] TURNER. Born, 1 Apr 1918, in Princeton, BC, Can. She married Carl S. SMITH, 3 Jun 1939. Resided, 1969, in Walla Walla, WA.

354 ii. Leslie Roy TURNER. Born, 11 May 1924, in Princeton, BC, Can.

256. **Charles Franklin[5] TURNER** (Jefferson Davis, 128). Born, 18 Dec 1885, in Hoggi, Columbia, WA. Died, 17 Apr 1953, in Pocatello, Bannock, ID, age 67. He was a homesteader and did wheat farming near Arbon, Power, ID.

He married Ruth Anna SPAIN, daughter of King SPAIN and Alma SPRAY, 10 Mar 1911. Born, 11 May 1895, in North Powder, Union, OR. Died, 13 Jan 1951, in Pocatello, Bannock, ID. They were on the 1920 Power, ID census. Children:[7]

+ 355 i. Zada Mae[6] TURNER.

+ 356 ii. Eunice Gladys TURNER.

+ 357 iii. Doris Frankie TURNER.

358 iv. Helen Larene TURNER. Born, 2 Apr 1917, in Arbon, Power, ID. Died, 18 Jul 1991. She married

W. Ralph JONES, son of Earl and Leota JONES. Born, Little Rock, AR. Died, 28 Apr 1991, Blackfoot, Bingham, ID.

+	359	v.	Alma Faye TURNER.
+	360	vi.	Charles Calvin TURNER.
+	361	vii.	Delmar Wayne TURNER.
+	362	viii.	Maralyn Joy TURNER.

257. **Myrtle Vivian^5 TURNER** (Jefferson Davis, 128). Born, 2 Apr 1887, in Columbia, WA. Died, 29 Dec 1959, in Dayton, Columbia, WA, age 72.

She married James Roy RANDOLPH, 10 Sep 1911, in Dayton, Columbia, WA. Born, 27 Nov 1883, in NE. Died, Aug 1965[8] or 21 Mar 1965 in Spokane, age 80.[9] They were on the 1920 census in Columbia, WA. Children:

363 i. Bonnie L.^{6} RANDOLPH. Born, 1913, in Dayton, Columbia, WA.

364 ii. Ronald R. RANDOLPH. Born, 1915, in Dayton, Columbia, WA.

258. **Harry Hill^5 TURNER** (Jefferson Davis, 128). Born, 15 Jan 1891, in Columbia, WA. Died, 22 Jun 1981, in Dayton, Columbia, WA, age 90.[10]

He married Lois May MITCHELL, 30 Sep 1914, in Dayton, Columbia, WA. Born, 11 May 1894, in Appleton City, St. Clair, MO. Died, 16 Oct 1971, in Dayton, Columbia, WA, age 77. Both are buried in the Dayton Cemetery. They were on the 1920 census in Franklin, WA. Children:[11]

+	365	i.	Harry Mitchell^6 TURNER.
+	366	ii.	Leslie Richard TURNER.
+	367	iii.	Donald Gene TURNER.
+	368	iv.	Lois June TURNER.

261. **Anita Emma^5 TURNER** (Jefferson Davis, 128). Born, 15 Feb 1895, in Columbia, WA. Died, 29 Nov 1985, in Aberdeen, Grays Harbor, WA, age 90.

She married Roy Lee CRALL, son of John Henry CRALL and Emma Alice KENDLE, 19 Dec 1913, in Dayton, Columbia, WA. Born, 2 Jun 1892, in Dayton, Columbia, WA. Died, 16 Aug 1978, in Hoquiam, Grays Harbor, WA, age 86. They are both buried at Hoquiam.[12] They were on the 1920 Dayton, Columbia, WA census. In 1969 they were living at Rt. 11, Box 612, Olympia, WA. Children:

369 i. Lois Lucille[6] CRALL. Born, 19 Dec 1913, in Dayton, Columbia, WA. She married, first, Joy Sherman MANNING. She married, second, Robert Holmes MCCOY, 27 Jul 1952, in Waitsburg, Walla Walla, WA.

370 ii. Erma Wave CRALL. Born, 7 Jan 1923, in Waitsburg, Walla Walla, WA. She married Ralph GILBERTSON, 13 April. Living 1993 at 503 Emerson Ave., Hoquiam, WA 98550.

262. **Zella Margaret[5] TURNER** (Jefferson Davis, 128). Born, 25 Oct 1896, in Columbia, WA. Died, 2 Sep 1974, in Dayton, Columbia, WA, buried in Tacoma, Pierce, WA, age 77.[13]

She married, first, Arthur HARTING, 1915, in Dayton, Columbia, WA. Born, 1895, WA. They were on the 1920 census in Dayton, Columbia, WA. Children:

371 i. Leo Arthur[6] HARTING. Born, 21 Oct 1916, in Dayton, Columbia, WA. Died, 18 Mar 1986, Walla Walla, WA, buried, Columbia, WA, age 69. He married Marcia May EAGER, 16 Jun 1941, in Dayton, Columbia, WA. Born, 6 Jun 1923. Died, 11 May 1988, Dayton, Columbia, WA, age 65.[14]

372 ii. Hubert R. HARTING. Born, 20 Apr 1919, in Dayton, Columbia, WA. Died, 29 Jan 1979, Dayton, Columbia, WA, age 59.[15]

She married, second, Prebble O. GROVE, 21 Dec 1944, in Tacoma, Pierce, WA. Born, 24 Jun 1880, in IL.

266. **Daisy Fern[5] TURNER** (Jefferson Davis, 128). Born, 10 May 1903, in Columbia, WA. Died, 3 Mar 1993, in Dayton, Columbia, WA, age 89.

She married Reade ABEL, son of Joel ABEL and Laura JOHNSON, Nov 1920, in Dayton, Columbia, WA. Born, 19 Mar 1898. Died, 27 May 1985, Dayton, Columbia, WA, age 87. They are both buried in the Dayton Cemetery. Reade ABEL worked as a very young man driving teams of mules and horses in harvest and then to Wenatchee to work in the fruit. Most of his later life he was a logger in Washington and Oregon.[16] Children:[17]

373 i. Loretta "Aleen"6 ABEL. Born, 27 Nov 1920. She married Loren C. SPOONEMORE, 26 Apr 1941, in Dayton, Columbia, WA. Born, 27 Mar 1915. Living at 308 W. Dayton Ave., Dayton WA 99328 in 1993.

283. **Marvin D.5 TURNER** (Edward Daniel, 132). Born, Nov 1896, in Nez Perce, ID. Died, 24 Mar 1964, in Caldwell, Canyon, ID, age 67. He served in World War I.

He married, Maude [UNKNOWN]. Children:

374 i. Buddy6 TURNER. Died, 6 yrs old.
\+ 375 ii. Carl TURNER.

284. **Melvin Verner5 TURNER** (Edward Daniel, 132). Born, 17 Nov 1897, in Frazier, Nez Perce, ID. Died of cancer, 21 Aug 1985, in Clarkston, Asotin, WA at the Tri-State Convalescent Center, age 87. He lived at Frazier until 1904 when his family moved to Kamiah. When he was 20 years old, he began farming at Mohler, halfway between Nezperce and Craigmont. He farmed there and at Nezperce until 1964 when he retired to Clarkston.[18]

He married, first, Vera Louise MOUGHMER, daughter of William MOUGHMER and Lenora RICHARDSON, 19 May 1927, in Lewiston, Nez Perce, ID. Born, 16 Sep 1904, at Cottonwood, Idaho, Idaho. Died of acute nephrosis after childbirth, 2 May 1934, at Lewiston, Nez Perce, ID, age 29. They are both buried at the Independent Order of Odd Fellows Cemetery at Craigmont. She went to Lewiston Normal School and graduated in 1925. She taught two years near Mohler in Lewis County, then married Melvin TURNER, a member of a pioneer family of that community. Her survivors were her husband, daughter, mother and sister, Mrs. Lenore MOUGHMER and Miss Venna MOUGHMER of Cottage Grove, OR.[19] Child:

\+ 376 i. Tona Rae^6 TURNER.

He married, second, Nancy Adilade BROWN, daughter of Charles W. BROWN and Jennie H. HUGGINS, 10 Apr 1936, Lewiston, Latah, ID. Born, 2 Apr 1911, Shawns, TN. Died of coronary disease, 14 Aug 1991, at Clarkston, Asotin, WA, age 80. Buried at Vineland Cemetery, Clarkston, WA. Her family moved to Culdesac, ID in the early 1920's and she graduated from high school there in 1929. In 1935 she graduated from Lewiston Normal School and taught at Webb Ridge School, southeast of Lewiston for a year before her marriage to Melvin V. TURNER. She was active in the Nezperce Christian Church and the Clarkston Christian Church.[20] Child:

\+ 377 ii. Melvin "Michael" TURNER.

285. **Otis Elgin^5 TURNER** (Edward Daniel, 132). Born, 15 Sep 1904, in Frazier, Nez Perce, ID. Died, 14 Feb 1985, Dinuba Tulare, CA, age 80.[21] He was living with his brother Melvin in Lewis Co., ID in 1920.

He married Della Judah DUNCAN, daughter of William Canady DUNCAN and Della Christina HALL, 19 Sep 1924, in Nezperce, ID. Born, 14 Apr 1903, in Thornton, Whitman, WA, moved with her parents to Craigmont, ID where she attended high school. Died from a stroke and complications of diabetes, 1 June 1978, age 75. They are both buried in the Smith Mountain Cemetery in Dinuba, Tulare, CA.[22]

Otis was a mail carrier and operated the General Store in Mohler when they were married. They lived over the store. Otis went to barber school and was a barber with Park LAW in Craigmont, ID. Around 1939 he was a partner in Earl BERRY'S general store at Craigmont and was a barber there until 1947 when he and his family moved to Dinuba, Tulare, CA. He was in the insurance business until he retired in 1969. Child:[23]

378 i. Diana "Diane" Gayle^6 TURNER. Born, 22 Feb 1933, Craigmont, Lewis, ID. She married, Ted AIVAZIAN, son of Hrant Ohan and Jane SAHAGIAN AIVAZIAN. Ted joined his father in the farming operation east of Reedley. He and Diane moved to the ranch in 1958 and in 1993 their address was 22319 E. Parlier, Reedley, CA 93654.

305. **Arthur Smith^5 TURNER** (James Arthur, 139). Born, 7 Nov 1893, in Clackamas, OR. Died, 18 Dec 1963, in Yakima, WA, age 70.[24] Buried in Dayton Cemetery, Columbia, WA.

He married Ada BURNELL, daughter of George Gardner BURNELL and Margaret WORTS, Born, 1 Oct 1904, in Fairview, British Columbia, Canada. Living in Dayton, WA in 1993.[25] Children:

+	379	i.	James Arthur^6 TURNER.
+	380	ii.	Lawrence Albert TURNER.

306. **Lloyd Julius^5 TURNER** (James Arthur, 139). Born, 16 Jul 1896, in Clackamas, OR. Died, 6 May 1957, in Fairview, British Columbia, Canada, age 61. Buried at the Dayton Cemetery.

He married Margaret BURNELL, daughter of George Gardner BURNELL and Margaret WORTS, 15 Mar 1924. Born, 18 Jul 1906, Fairview, British Columbia, Canada. Children:[26]

+	381	i.	Margaret Elaine^6 TURNER.
+	382	ii.	Marian Nadine TURNER.
+	383	iii.	Darline "Kae" TURNER.
	384	iv.	Lloyd George TURNER. Born, 22 Feb 1933, in Turner, Columbia, WA. Died, 13 Aug 1937, age 4.
	385	v.	Charles Lowell TURNER. Born, 16 Sep 1938, Dayton, in Columbia, WA. He married Patricia PRICE, daughter of Dennis PRICE, 9 Jun 1957 at the Methodist Church in Dayton, WA. She died and was buried at the Dayton Cemetery, 24 Jan 1981, age 41. He married, second, Nancy WADE BARTON.

307. **Lillie Nancy Otillia^5 TURNER** (James Arthur, 139). Born, Nov 1899, in Clackamas, OR. Died, 30 Jun 1940, Columbia, WA, age 41. Buried in the Dayton Cemetery.

She married Winifred "Fred" M. BROWER, 1919. Born, 1897, in WA and lived in Milton, Umatilla, OR. They were on the 1920 Columbia, WA census. Children:[27]

386	i.	Lily M.^{6} BROWER. Born, 1920, OR.
387	ii.	Zelma BROWER. She married Delbert

WEATHERMAN. Resided, 1993, 1855 Highland Rd., Walla Walla, WA 99362.

388 iii. Patsy BROWER. She married [Unknown] GRIFFIN. Resided, 1975, in Waitsburg, Walla Walla, WA.

389 iv. May BROWER. Resided, 1975, in MT.

309. **Gladys Ellen^5 TURNER** (James Arthur, 139). Born, 24 Dec 1904, in Turner, Columbia, WA.

She married Wayne JONES, 1920. Child:[28]

390 i. Bettie^6 JONES. She married [Unknown] RICE. Resided, 1975, in Lewiston, Nez Perce, ID.

310. **Hattie Maye^5 TURNER** (James Arthur, 139). Born, 2 Aug 1907, in Turner, Columbia, WA. Died, 9 Jul 1931, Dayton, Columbia, WA, age 23.[29] She was buried in the Dayton Cemetery.

She married Benjamin Curtis DARNELL, 28 Sep 1925, in Dayton, Columbia, WA. Born, 24 Nov 1901. Died, 16 Oct 1956. Children:[30]

391 i. Maxine May^6 DARNELL. Born, 18 Nov 1927. She married Ray Z. MUNDEN, 1949. Born 17 Dec 1924. Died, 7 Dec 1968.

392 ii. Dorothy DARNELL. Died, 24 Jan 1930, Walla Walla, WA.

311. **Thomas Jeffries^5 TURNER** (James Arthur, 139). Born, 29 Mar 1911, in Dayton, Columbia, WA. Died, 16 Apr 1976, in Dayton, Columbia, WA, age 65. Buried in the Dayton Cemetery. Tom and his sister Goldie operated the Dayton Cleaners until they retired in 1973.[31]

He married Agnes HUFF, 29 Nov 1947. Children:

393 i. Bruce^6 TURNER. Born, circa 1952, in Columbia, WA.

394 ii. Jan TURNER. Born, circa 1954, in Columbia, WA.

NOTES: CHAPTER 5 - FIFTH GENERATION

---

[1] Rinehart, *Covello*, pp. 70, 286, 291.
[2] Ewing, *My Turner Family*, p. 4.
[3] *Ibid.*, p. 5.
[4] Information on this family supplied by Altha L. SMITH, 1812 Evergreen St., Walla Walla, WA 99362, in 1969.
[5] Information on this family supplied by Irene BARGER, 20 S. Clinton, Walla Walla, WA, in 1967 and 1968.
[6] Letter from Altha L. SMITH, in 1969.
[7] Letters from Alma GOWER, 2083 Quail Ave, Yuma AZ 85364, 29 Sep 1993, 25 Oct 1993.
[8] Social Security File.
[9] Washington State Death Index.
[10] Social Security File and Washington State Death Index.
[11] Letter from H. H. TURNER, 416 E. Clay, Dayton, WA, 25 Jan 1968 and Washington State Death Index.
[12] Both death records are in the Social Security File and in the Washington State Death Index.
[13] Social Security File and Washington State Death Index.
[14] Washington State Death Index.
[15] Washington State Death Index.
[16] Letter from Aleen SPOONEMORE, 308 W. Dayton, Dayton, WA 99328, 30 July 1993.
[17] Rinehart, *Covello*, p. 71.
[18] Social Security File; Obituary.
[19] Obituary from the *Nezperce Herald*, 10 May 1934, and the *Lewiston Morning Tribune*, 3 May 1934, Funeral Record.
[20] Obituary from unknown paper, 14 Aug 1991.
[21] Social Security File.
[22] Social Security File, Obituary from the *Lewiston Morning Tribune*, 5 June 1978.
[23] Information on this family from Diane AIVAZIAN, 21 July 1993.
[24] Washington State Death Index.
[25] Social Security File and Washington State Death Index.
[26] Information on this family from Kae FLETCHER, 4 Dec 1993, Rinehart, *Covello*, p. 70.
[27] *Ibid.*
[28] *Ibid.*, p. 71.
[29] Obituary from the *Columbia County News*.
[30] Rinehart, *Covello*, p. 71.
[31] *Ibid.*, pp. 70-71.

CHAPTER 6

THE SIXTH GENERATION

337. Hazel G.[6] TURNER (William H., 169). Born, 2 Jul 1899, in MO. Died, 2 Mar 1919, in MO, age 19.

She married Wesley W. BRECKINRIDGE, 14 May 1918, in MO. The children were living with their TURNER grandparents on the 1920 census in Wyaconda, Clark, MO. Children:

395 i. Hazel Jean[7] BRECKINRIDGE. Born, 2 Mar 1919. She married Russell CRAVENS of Memphis, MO.
396 ii. William Wesley BRECKINRIDGE. Born, 2 Mar 1919. Married.

346. Vivian Irene[6] TURNER (Grover Thomas, 232). Born, 9 Jan 1920, in Mission City, BC, Can. Vivian MCCAULEY living (1993) at 214 N 2nd St., Dayton, WA.[1]

She married, first, Dick GRENFELL.

She married, second, Paul F. ESLICK. Born, 1921. Died, 14 Jun 1965, age 44. Buried at the Dayton Cemetery. Children:

397 i. Richard Henry[7] GRENFELL ESLICK. Born, 4 Jul 1942. He married Vicki TEWALT.
398 ii. Susan Rene ESLICK. Born, 24 Jan 1948. She married Dwight RICHTER.

She married, third, Dean SHEA.

She married, fourth, MCCAULEY.

347. Laura Jean[6] TURNER (Grover Thomas, 232). Born, 15 Jan 1922, in Dixie, Columbia, WA. Living (1993) at 341 S.W. Meritt Lane, Madras, OR 97741.

She married, first, Claire YOUNG. Child:

399 i. Gary Lee[7] YOUNG. Born, 21 Dec 1942. He married Sharon MILLER. Living (1993) at 148 Main St., Dayton, WA 99328.

She married, second, David Lloyd DAVIDSON. Children:

400 ii. Cynthia DAVIDSON. Born, 26 Jul 1953. She married Terry ROBINS.
401 iii. Loran DAVIDSON. Born, Feb 1963.
402 iv. Michele DAVIDSON. Born, Aug 1965.

348. Grover Robert[6] TURNER (Grover Thomas, 232). Born, 15 Sep 1925, in Telhwa, BC, Canada.

He married Margaret MCBRIDE. Children:

403 i. Michael[7] TURNER. Born, circa 1945, in WA.
404 ii. Jeffrey TURNER. Born, circa 1947, in WA.
405 iii. Cheryl TURNER. Born, 5 Jul 1949, in WA.

349. Ben Delbert[6] TURNER (Grover Thomas, 232). Born, 14 Jul 1929, in Telhwa, BC, Can. Living (1993) at Box 192, Ilwaco, WA 98624.

He married Elna BOZELEY. Children:

406 i. Linda[7] TURNER. Born, circa 1950, in WA.
407 ii. Debra TURNER. Born, circa 1952, in WA.
408 iii. Ben Delbert TURNER. Born, circa 1954, in WA.
409 iv. Tonia TURNER. Born, circa 1956, in WA.

351. Thomas Lee[6] TURNER (Grover Thomas, 232). Born, 9 Sep 1934, in Dayton, Columbia, WA. Living (1993) at Portland Mobile Court, 9000 N.E. Union, Portland, OR 97211.

He married Carol [UNKNOWN]. Children:

410 i. Nanette[7] TURNER. Born, circa 1955, in WA.
411 ii. Brian TURNER. Born, circa 1957, in WA.
412 iii. Danny TURNER.

355. Zada Mae[6] TURNER (Charles Franklin, 256). Born, 10 Apr 1912, in Hot Springs, OR.

She married Earl E. HUNT, May 1933, in Pocatello, Bannock, ID. Born, in Waco, TX. Died, San Leandro, Alameda, CA. Children:

413 i. Leonard Earl[7] HUNT. Born, 1 May 1934, in Pocatello, Bannock, ID. He married Margaret SKINNER, 18 Mar 1960. He is a Realtor.

414 ii. Gary Dee HUNT. Born, 30 Apr 1935. He married, first, Theresa [UNKNOWN], 1 Oct 1960. He is a Realtor in San Leandro, CA.

356. Eunice Gladys[6] TURNER (Charles Franklin, 256). Born, 24 May 1913, in Arbon, Power, ID.

She married Leslie HUNT, Pocatello, Bannock, ID. Born, in Waco, TX. Died, Pocatello, Bannock, ID. He worked at the Rail Road shops. He was the brother of Earl HUNT. Children:

415 i. James Leslie[7] HUNT. Born, 28 Dec 1931, in Pocatello, Bannock, ID. Died, Anaheim, Orange, CA.

416 ii. Kenneth Earl HUNT. Born, 12 Dec 1932, in Pocatello, Bannock, ID.

417 iii. Gail Dean HUNT. Born, 26 Nov 1934, in Pocatello, Bannock, ID. Died.

418 iv. Dixie Lee HUNT. Born, 26 Apr 1941, in Pocatello, Bannock, ID. She married Lamar ROBINSON. They live at Eagle, Ada, ID where he is employed by Idaho Water Power Company.

419 vi. Douglas Franklin HUNT. Born, 12 Apr 1944, in Pocatello, Bannock, ID.

357. Doris Frankie[6] TURNER (Charles Franklin, 256). Born, 22 Feb 1915, in Arbon, Power, ID.

She married Robert ROBINSON. Born, 8 Jul 1920. Died, Aug 1990, Pocatello, Bannock, ID. Retired from INEL at Arco. Children:

420 i. Byron Kent[7] ROBINSON. Born, 3 Nov 1951. Died, Pocatello, Bannock, ID.

421 ii. Calvin W. ROBINSON. Born, 7 Nov 1952. Died, Pocatello, Bannock, ID.

359. Alma Faye[6] TURNER (Charles Franklin, 256). Born, 12 Apr 1919, in Union, Union, OR. Resided, 1993, at 2083 Quail Ave, Yuma, AZ 85364. She was a Civil Service Clerk Typist and a Certified N. A. & Seamstress.[2]

She married, first, Walfred Robert BERGSTROM, son of Otto Walfred BERGSTROM and Freda J. ANDERSON, 14 Nov 1945, in Spokane, Spokane, WA. Born, 5 Mar 1920, in Sandpoint, Bonner, ID. Died, 9 Jan 1976. He was a Pharmacist. Children:

422 i. Sheryl Justine[7] BERGSTROM. Born, 30 Sep 1947, in Pocatello, Bannock, ID. She married Randall HENLEY. She is a High School French Teacher in Boise, Ada, ID.

423 ii. Signa Kristine BERGSTROM. Born, 6 Dec 1950, in Coeur d'Alene, Kootenai, ID. She married Alan D. REASOR. She is a Registered Nurse in Boise, Ada, ID..

424 iii. Roberta Arlene Faye BERGSTROM. Born, 12 Jan 1955, in Coeur d'Alene, Kootenai, ID. She married Bruce SCOTT. She is a Micro Biologist in Boise, Ada, ID..

She married, second, Harold GOWER. Died, 17 Nov 1992, Yuma, Yuma, AZ. Cremated and sent to Spokane, WA.

360. Charles Calvin[6] TURNER (Charles Franklin, 256). Born, 14 Sep 1925, in Arbon, Power, ID. Died, 21 Nov 1986, American Falls, Power, ID. He was a veteran of World War II and a Captain in the Navy C. Bs. He retired from Simplot Company.

He married Eleanor PACKER, 1958, at Pocatello, Bannock, ID. Children:

425 i. Joyce R.[7] TURNER. Born, 14 Feb 1960, in American Falls, Power, ID. She married Jay FOSTER.

426 ii. Janet F. TURNER. Born, 2 Aug 1962, in American Falls, Power, ID. She married Robert BURNELLE.

\+ 427 iii. Charles Lyndon TURNER.

\+ 428 iv. Ronald G. TURNER.

361. Delmar Wayne[6] TURNER (Charles Franklin, 256). Born, 12 Jul 1928, in Arbon, Power, ID. He was a Big Equipment Operator for Construction Engineers and retired on disability. They live at Rt. #2, Box 5G, Lenore, ID 83541.

He married Darlene J. BUCKENDORF, daughter of John W. BUCKENDORF and Mary Ellen JONES, 11 Mar 1950, in Blackfoot, Bingham, ID. Born, 18 Dec 1932, Pocatello, Bannock, ID. Children:

	429	i.	Deborah Lynne[7] TURNER. Born, 1 Sep 1951, in Portland, Multnomah, OR. She married Jim EVANS.
+	430	ii.	Darla Kaye TURNER.
+	431	iii.	Floyd Dale TURNER.

362. Maralyn Joy[6] TURNER (Charles Franklin, 256). Born, 18 Sep 1936, in Pocatello, Bannock, ID. She is a retired Assistant Manager from Safeway.

She married Joseph LaNae MURDOCK, son of Joseph Grant MURDOCK and Sarah Ora GRIFFITHS, 6 Jun 1957, in Pocatello, Bannock, ID. Born, 11 Jan 1932, in Cedar City, Iron, UT. He is a retired Operating Construction Engineer. Children:

432	i.	Kevin LaNae[7] MURDOCK. Born, 24 May 1960, in Council, Adams, ID.
433	ii.	Kirk Charles MURDOCK. Born, 6 Sep 1963, in Boise, Ada, ID.
434	iii.	Kandis Joy MURDOCK. Born, 8 Jun 1966, in Council, Adams, ID. She married Todd ROMANS of Boise, Ada, ID.

365. Harry Mitchell[6] TURNER (Harry Hill, 258). Born, 21 Jun 1915, in Dayton, Columbia, WA.

He married Lenora Jean PAYNE, daughter of Louis Garland PAYNE and Edith Lenora FRY, 23 Jun 1940, in Lewiston, Nez Perce, ID. Born, 20 Jun 1919, in Waitsburg, Walla Walla, WA. They live in Dayton, WA in 1993. Children:

435	i.	Laurel Anne[7] TURNER. Born, 8 Jun 1949, in Dayton, Columbia, WA. She married, first, Richard Thomas BROWN, 23 Feb 1966. She married, second, [Unknown] GOODWATER. They live in Dayton, Columbia, WA.
436	ii.	Larry Mitchell TURNER. Born, 18 Jun 1954, in Dayton, Columbia, WA. He lives in Pasco, Franklin, WA.

366. Leslie Richard^6 TURNER (Harry Hill, 258). Born, 17 Apr 1917, in Dayton, Columbia, WA. Died, 22 Apr 1982, Dayton, Columbia, WA, age 65.[3] Buried in the Dayton Cemetery.

He married, first, Mary FRANK, Mar 1940. Child:

437 i. John David^7 TURNER. Born, 1947.

He married, second, Laura [UNKNOWN]. Child:

438 ii. Cindy TURNER. She married [Unknown] ROBBINS.

367. Donald Gene^6 TURNER (Harry Hill, 258). Born, 16 Mar 1924, in Pasco, Franklin, WA. He is a retired Lt. Col., U. S. Air Force and was a pilot in three wars. Resides (1993) at Rt. 3, Box 590, Dayton, WA 99328.[4]

He married Ula Mae HILLHOUSE, daughter of Jim HILLHOUSE and Nina BALDRIDGE, 30 Sep 1944, in Lubbock, Lubbock, TX. Born, 3 Dec 1923, in Dayton, Columbia, WA. Children:

\+ 439 i. Gene Merlene^7 TURNER.
\+ 440 ii. Gale Ardene TURNER.

368. Lois June^6 TURNER (Harry Hill, 258). Born, 3 Dec 1927, in Pasco, Franklin, WA.

She married, first, Robert WALKER, 1943. Children:

441 i. Leslie Duane^7 WALKER. Born, 1946.
442 ii. Leana WALKER. Born, 1947. Died, Jan 1992, age 44.

She married, second, Jack DAVIS. Child:

443 iii. Diane DAVIS. Born, 24 Feb 1950. She married [Unknown] ENGH. They live in Moses Lake, Grant, WA. (1993)

She married, third, Jim HUBNER. They live in Post Falls, Kootenai, ID. Children:

444 iv. Son.
445 v. Daughter.

375. Carl^{6} TURNER (Marvin D., 283). Lived in Caldwell, Canyon, ID.

He married, first, Rita [UNKNOWN]. Children:

446 i. Rodney^{7} TURNER. Killed in Vietnam, 18 years old.
447 ii. Debbie TURNER. Living in ID.

He married, second, M. A., living at W. 1307 Alice, Spokane, WA in 1993.

376. Tona Rae^{6} TURNER (Melvin Verner, 284). Born, 28 Apr 1934, Lewiston, Nez Perce, ID.[5]

She married, Edward Neil STACH, son of Joseph Nicholas STACH and Mary Cecilia MONTAGUE of Nez Perce, 31 Oct 1954, in Moscow, Latah, ID at the Saint Mary's Catholic Church. Born, 15 Jul 1930, Nez Perce, Lewis, ID. He works for the Gear Works in South Park. They are presently living at 11735 SE 78th Pl., Renton, King, WA. 98056. (1993) Children:

448 i. Anita Rae^{7} STACH. Born, 15 Apr 1955, Cottonwood, Idaho, ID. She married, Brian HALEY, 5 Nov 1977, Seattle, King, WA.
449 ii. Lori Therese STACH. Born, 20 Jan 1957, Cottonwood, Idaho, ID. She married, Gerald Lawrence DORN, 26 Jun 1979, Seattle, King, WA.
450 iii. Dean Michael STACH. Born, 17 Jul 1961, Spokane, Spokane, WA. He married, Theresa RIEWOLD, 26 Oct 1991, Seattle, King, WA.
451 iv. Julie STACH. Born, 21 Jan 1964, Seattle, King, WA.

377. Melvin "Michael"^{6} TURNER (Melvin Verner, 284). Born, 27 Jun 1939, Craigmont, Lewis, ID. Living at 1424 Chestnut St., Milton Freewater, OR 97862 in 1993. He is retired from the Union Pacific Railroad and is part owner of TURNER-STACH farming.[6]

He married, first, Diana Lee HILL, daughter of Cecil and Martha HILL, Feb 1960, Moscow, Latah, ID. Born, 1941, Lewiston, Nez Perce, ID. Children:

+ 452 i. Carmen Sue^{7} TURNER.

+ 453 ii. Joanna Kay TURNER.

She married, second, Roger MILLER, third, Johnny SMATHERS.

He married, second, Karen Mae UHLENKOTT, Jul 1969, Lewiston, Nez Perce, ID. Born, 15 Oct 1939, Lewiston, Nezperce, ID. Died, 14 Sep 1980, Spokane, WA. Buried at Lewiston, ID. Child:

454 iii. Robert Michael TURNER. Born, 19 Jun 1971, Downey, Los Angeles, CA. He is in the Air Force.

He married, third, Sherry WILLIAMS, daughter of John J. and Kathern B. WILLIAMS, 15 May 1980. Born, 31 Jul 1948, Twin Falls, Twin Falls, ID. Michael adopted her son.

455 iv. Travis John TURNER. Born, 20 Oct 1971, Twin Falls, ID. He is in the Marines.

379. James Arthur^6 TURNER (Arthur Smith, 305). Born, 1 May 1926, in Turner, Columbia, WA. Resided, 1993 in Turner, Columbia, WA where he farmed 2,572 acres with his brother Lawrence and their two sons and had formed a partnership called "TURNER Brothers." The TURNER Brothers operated five self-propelled combines and the trucks necessary to handle the wheat. They won the Conservation Farmer of the Year award given by the Dayton Kiwanis Club.[7]

He married, first, Patricia CALAHAN, 21 Feb 1949. Born, 6 Dec 1927. Died, 12 Dec 1985. Child:

456 i. Randy Lane^7 TURNER. Born, 14 May 1951, in Dayton, Columbia, WA. Resided, 1993, RR#3, Dayton, WA 99328.

He married, second, Laura BERRY, May 1986.

380. Lawrence Albert^6 TURNER (Arthur Smith, 305). Born, 21 Feb 1928, in Turner, Columbia, WA. Resided, 1975, in Turner, Columbia, WA where he was serving his second term as County Commissioner. These two TURNER families (Lawrence and his brother James) represent over 100 years of farming in Columbia County by the TURNER family.

He married Betty LAUGHERY, daughter of Marvin LAUGHERY and Christine HATFIELD, 17 Jul 1948. Born, 21 May 1931, Dayton, Columbia, WA. Child:

+ 457 i. Richard Dean^{7} TURNER.

381. Margaret Elaine^{6} TURNER. (Lloyd Julius, 306). Born, 4 Oct 1924, in Turner, Columbia, WA.[8]

She married Keith Spencer LUNSFORD, son of Lawson Kilgore LUNSFORD and Carma SPENCER, 24 Nov 1945, Woodruff, Rich, UT. Born, 3 Nov 1923, in Evanston, Uinta, WY. Resided, 1993, in Lakewood, CO. Children:

458 i. Stephen Spencer^{7} LUNSFORD. Born, 22 Oct 1946, in Great Falls, Cascade, MT. He married, Shannon Rae HUDSON, daughter of Fred Edwin HUDSON and Shirley Rose CLARK, 28 Apr 1973, Casper, Natrona, WY. Born, 21 Jun 1950, in Lander, Fremont, WY.

459 ii. Michael Turner LUNSFORD. Born, 16 Dec 1947, in Evanston, Uinta, WY. Died, 16 Dec 1947.

460 iii. Vicki Lynn LUNSFORD. Born, 20 Oct 1949, in Jackson, Teton, WY. She married, Steven V. PARKS, son of Cecil Alfred PARKS and Patty CAREY. Born, 30 Nov 1952, in Eugene, Lane, OR. Divorced.

461 iv. Adrienne Gaile LUNSFORD. Born, 21 Apr 1953, in Casper, Natrona, WY. She married, James F. TAYLOR, son of Charles L. TAYLOR and Geraldine L. PETERSON, 15 Feb 1986, Littleton, Arapahoe, CO. Born, 30 May 1950, in Waynesburg, Greene, PA.

462 v. Leigh Ann LUNSFORD. Born, 17 Dec, 1955, in Casper, Natrona, WY. She married, Michael SLAUGHTER, son of Melvin SLAUGHTER and Lois ADAY, 23 Aug 1980, Golden, Jefferson, CO. Born, 10 Oct 1957, in El Centro, Imperial, CA.

463 vi. Evan Turner LUNSFORD. Born, 17 Feb 1961, in Casper, Natrona, WY. He married, Patricia Gail GRANT, daughter of Harold GRANT and Barbara WARBURTON, 10 Jan 1981, Denver, Denver, CO. Born, 29 Jan 1960.

464 vii. Margaret Louise LUNSFORD. Born, 9 Feb 1966, in Casper, Natrona, WY.

382. Marian Nadine[6] TURNER (Lloyd Julius, 306). Born, 1 Sep 1926, in Turner, Columbia, WA.

She married Joseph Keith STARTIN, 4 Nov 1950. Born, 7 Apr 1926, in Dayton, Columbia, WA. Resided, 1993, 618 S. 6th St., Dayton, WA 99328.

"The STARTIN family came from Kansas in the early days and settled on the mountain south of Dittemore on the Patit. Later they bought the Tom REED place (618 acres)."[9] Children:

465 i. Cathy Jo[7] STARTIN. Born, 16 Sep 1960, in Puyallup, Pierce, WA. She married first, Scott CHARPENTEIR. Divorced. She married second, Dave WOODALL. Born, 9 Sep 1960, in White Salmon, Klickitat, WA.

466 ii. Thomas Keith STARTIN. Born, 8 Feb 1963, in Tacoma, Pierce, WA. He married, Tina CLEVELAND. Born, 17 Mar 1963.

383. Darline "Kae"[6] TURNER (Lloyd Julius, 306). Born, 28 Nov 1930, in Dayton, Columbia, WA.

She married Russell Eugene FLETCHER, 20 Mar 1948, in Columbia, WA. Born, 13 Jul 1919. Resided, 1993, RR#3, Dayton, WA 99328. Children:

467 i. David Eugene[7] FLETCHER. Born, 10 Jun 1949. He married, Mary K. EGGER, 5 Jun 1982.

468 ii. Michael Lee FLETCHER. Born, 9 Sep 1950. He married, Jeannie BOGGS. Divorced.

469 iii. Allen Ray FLETCHER. Born, 25 Mar 1952. He married, Yvette Fae DIEU, daughter of Thomas Anthony DIEU and Patricia Ann MARLL, 26 Jun 1990. Born, 26 Apr 1971.

470 iv. James Andrew FLETCHER. Born 22 Jan 1954. He married, Janette PATTON, 21 Dec 1983.

471 v. Linda Kae FLETCHER. Born, 14 Sep 1956. She married, Curtis Owen COOMBS, son of Chester COOMBS and Dona SCOTT, 18 Dec 1976. Born, 15 Apr 1958.

CHAPTER 7

THE SEVENTH GENERATION

427. **Charles Lyndon[7] TURNER** (Charles Calvin, 360). Born, 20 Jun 1965, in American Falls, Power, ID. They live at Nampa, Canyon, ID in 1993.

He married Elizabeth [UNKNOWN]. Children:

472 i. Wess[8] TURNER.
473 ii. Travis TURNER.

428. **Ronald G.[7] TURNER** (Charles Calvin, 360). Born, 10 Nov 1967, in American Falls, Power, ID. He is a Welder living at Arbon, Power, ID in 1993.

He married Ginger CRANE. Child:

474 i. Brittainy[8] TURNER.

430. **Darla Kaye[7] TURNER** (Delmar Wayne, 361). Born, 10 Apr 1953, in Pocatello, Bannock, ID. Lives at Aloha, Washington, OR (1993).

She married Wesley FISHER. Children:

475 i. Ashley E.[8] FISHER.
476 ii. Joel W. FISHER.
477 iii. Hanna E. FISHER.

431. **Floyd Dale[7] TURNER** (Delmar Wayne, 361). Born, 20 Sep 1954, in Pocatello, Bannock, ID. Lives in Lapwai, Nez Perce, ID (1993).

He married, first, [UNKNOWN], from Orofino, Clearwater, ID. She lives at Grand Junction, Mesa, CO. Children:

478 i. Randy[8] TURNER.
479 ii. Kelley TURNER.

He married, second, Debbie [UNKNOWN].

439. **Gene Merlene**[7] **TURNER** (Donald Gene, 367). Born, 10 Mar 1946, in Dayton, Columbia, WA.

She married, first, Robert Steven MCMUNN, 1 Aug 1963. Child:

480 i. Lori Jean[8] MCMUNN. Born, 4 Mar 1960. She married [Unknown] WALLISER. Resided, 1993, in Spokane, WA, where she is an Interior Decorator.

She married, second, Jon WOLF, 12 Jan 1985.

440. **Gale Ardene**[7] **TURNER** (Donald Gene, 367). Born, 14 Jun 1955, in Dayton, Columbia, WA.

She married Lainie OPP, 20 Apr 1980. Children:

481 i. Chelsea Dawn[8] OPP. Born, 14 Nov 1983.
482 ii. Bethany Dyan OPP. Born, 30 Nov 1986.

452. **Carmen Sue**[7] **TURNER** (Melvin "Michael," 377). Born, 15 Feb 1961, Moscow, Latah, ID.

She married Jay TAYLOR, Lewiston, Nezperce, ID. They live in Lewiston, ID (1993). Children:

483 i. Son.[8]
484 ii. Daughter.

453. **Joanna Kay**[7] **TURNER** (Melvin "Michael," 377). Born, 10 Jan 1963, Coeur d'Alene, Kootenai, ID.

She married Jeff WHITLEY, Reno, Washoe, NE. They live in McMinnville, Yamhill, OR (1993). Child:

485 i. Daughter.[8]

457. **Richard Dean**[7] **TURNER** (Lawrence Albert, 380). Born, 15 Dec 1951, in Dayton, Columbia, WA. Resided (1993) RR#3, Dayton, WA 99328.

He married Valerie Gay HAWARD, daughter of Donald HAWARD and Janet HOURUD. Born, 19 Feb 1959, Dayton, Columbia, WA. Children:

486 i. Benjamin Lawrence[8] TURNER. Born, 3 Feb 1984.
487 ii. Rachel Dawn TURNER. Born, 16 Mar 1988.

NOTES: CHAPTER 6 - SIXTH GENERATION
NOTES: CHAPTER 7 - SEVENTH GENERATION

---

1 Information from Vivian MCCAULEY, 1993.
2 Information from Alma GOWER, 29 Sep 1993.
3 Social Security File and Washington State Death Index.
4 Information from Donald TURNER, 30 Sep 1993.
5 Information from Tona Rae STACH, 1993.
6 Information from Michael TURNER, 1993.
7 Rinehart, *Covello*, pp. 70, 264, 296.
8 Information on all of the family of Lloyd Julius TURNER from Kae FLETCHER, 4 Dec 1993.
9 Rinehart, *Covello*, p. 93.

FINIS

THE DESCENDANTS OF JOHN MERIDY TURNER (1737-1815)
OF FAUQUIER COUNTY, VIRGINIA

NAME INDEX

Women are indexed by both their maiden name and their married name. In many cases, more than one entry for the same name can be found on the page indicated.

www.ingramcontent.com/pod-product-compliance
Lightning Source LLC
Chambersburg PA
CBHW070839300326
41935CB00038B/1154

9780788401459